dadima's

Celebrating Grandmother's Wisdom
Through Indian Cooking

anneeka ludhra

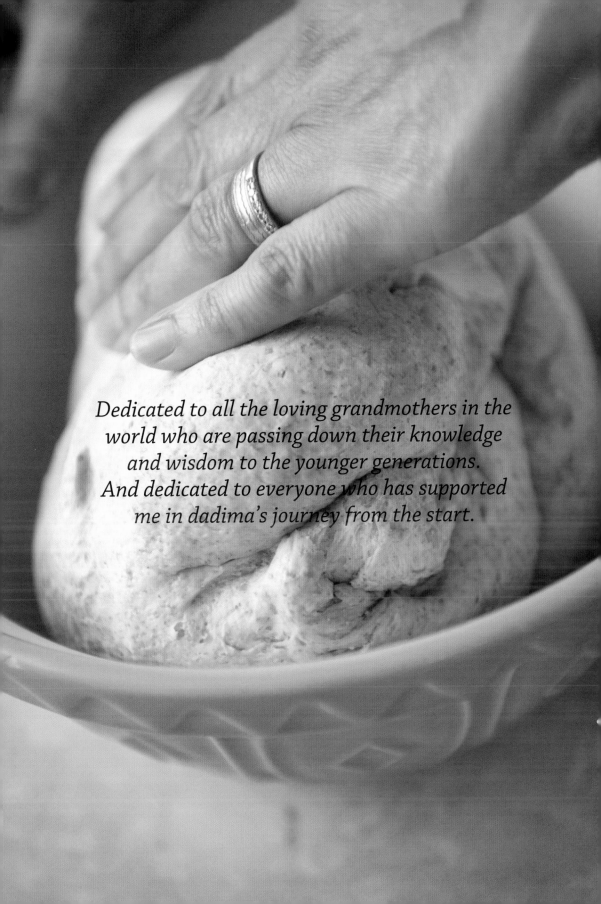

Dedicated to all the loving grandmothers in the world who are passing down their knowledge and wisdom to the younger generations. And dedicated to everyone who has supported me in dadima's journey from the start.

First published in Great Britain in 2016 on behalf of:
Dadima's – www.dadimas.co.uk

Published by:
RMC Media – www.rmcmedia.co.uk
6 Broadfield Court, Sheffield, S8 0XF
Tel: 0114 250 6300

Text © Anneeka Ludhra, 2016
Layout and design © RMC Media, 2016
Photography © Tim Green (www.timgreenphotographer.co.uk), 2016

Editor: Adam Kay
Design: Richard Abbey
Proofreader: Christopher Brierley

Printed and bound in Malta by:
Gutenberg Press Ltd – www.gutenberg.com.mt
Gudja Road, Tarxien, Malta, GXQ 2902
Tel: 00356 2189 7037

A CIP catalogue record for this book is available from the British Library.

ISBN: 978-1-907998-25-6

Dadima – *the Hindi noun for a father's mother; the English equivalent of grandmother.*

his cookery book is called dadima's – grandmother's. To clarify, although I have chosen to use the Hindi word for grandmother, this is because there is not a single noun which refers to both a maternal and paternal grandmother. My point is I use the title dadima's, which refers to a paternal grandmother. However, my book makes an equal tribute to nanima's (nan's). I've chosen to use a possessive apostrophe on dadima's book title. Whilst the book is a celebration of grandmothers collectively (dadimas), I value each grandmother for her unique approach (dadima's).

This book is about traditional Indian recipes, which were shared with me over a period of time by very experienced dadimas. They all have a passion for cooking, and feeding their immediate and extended families and friends. These dadimas welcomed me into their homes and hearts, and it was an absolute privilege to learn from them. They shared with me their culinary journeys and knowledge of Indian cooking, and they talked to me about significant moments in their lives. These dadimas all stated how the process of participating in my book research was a first time for them in talking through their food journeys and associated life events. This made my journey of learning even more special. As a keen pupil learns from their teacher, I studied first-hand each dadima's techniques and cooking philosophies. I discovered the secrets which had been passed down to them by their elders. As I listened and learned, I grew to love and understand each dadima's unique style, and gradually unlock for myself the key to her cooking success. It wasn't easy and it took lots of practice and mastery, although they made it look effortless!

Indian cooking is a melting pot of eclectic styles and flavours, with recipes for particular dishes varying between regions. It would be a sweeping generalisation, then, to say that the dishes in this book are representative of Indian cooking as a whole. Like other cuisines, the beauty of Indian food is in its regional culinary identities. The seven special dadimas featured in this book cook with North Indian Punjabi influences, combined with their culinary secrets, particularly tailored to their family's tastes. Even then, their cooking will not necessarily be representative of Punjabi cooking, as each family has their own preferences and interpretations of what 'authentic' means to them. As readers, you may look at a particular recipe and think 'Well, my dadima (or gran) doesn't do it like that – she usually does this.' This kind of response delights me, as it reminds me of the very reason that I chose to spell 'dadima's' with an apostrophe. Each dadima's cooking is individual to her and her family. I encourage you to add your own individual touches to each recipe, just like I have when cooking and tweaking their dishes. Being creative is the real fun of it, and dadima's is all about 'connecting generations' through lots of talking, listening and learning.

My dadima was the inspiration for the concept behind this book. Passionate about cooking for her family, she is the ultimate Mother Nature figure. She does not work in a Michelin-star restaurant, or appear on television, but in her very special way, she is our family's celebrity chef. My dadima's traditional cooking is a precious family heirloom, her dishes have stood the test of time, and are now being enjoyed by her great-grandchildren. Most importantly, her cooking contains years of rich stories and life experiences, which include hardship, resilience, faith and hope. Her food is so much more than just great food – it is full of love, wisdom and kindness.

I've always loved cooking with my mother from a young age, and she promoted home-cooked food as always being the best option. As children, we didn't eat out in many restaurants; my dadima would always cook for the family. Every dish I share with you in this book is based on, or inspired by, a recipe that I have learnt from one of my talented dadimas. I use 'my' here as it feels like they have all become my dadimas in their own special way. These seven inspirational women found pleasure in others enjoying their food, and always found time to cook, however busy their lives were. I have learnt how to cook their dishes, drawing on their tried and tested techniques and recipes as a starting point. Their recipes were generally not written down, but all remembered through experience and memory. I have added some of my own 'modern' twists here and there, and these tweaks will hopefully suit the pressures of a busy modern lifestyle, yet nurture a love for entertaining and sharing food at home.

As a granddaughter, it's been important for me to make time to learn from my grandmother, and other talented women of her generation.

My early childhood experiences have influenced the thinking behind this book. As a young girl, I lived with my dadima for the first four years of my life, and then moved to an area with mainly retired and elderly people. Our retired neighbours had lots of time to talk to me, and I loved talking! Some would even babysit us when mum was busy, and I would spend hours with them, learning about their histories and their experiences of war, and watching them bake and cook with simple ingredients, including home-grown fruit and vegetables from their well-tended gardens. These early experiences must have inspired me to capture the legacies of 'ordinary' women, as to me, they seemed extraordinary. The dadimas featured in this book are hard-working, resilient, and incredibly giving of their time, love and energy.

So who am I? Well, I'm not a celebrity chef or restaurant owner, but I've been told that I'm a pretty good cook. I'm an ordinary girl with a dream to develop a new concept that is very close to my heart, embedded in the values of my upbringing. I believe in celebrating the wisdom of our elders – they can be our best 'libraries' if we take some time to learn from them. I have been fortunate to travel from a young age, and have always been drawn to interesting people, learning new languages, and exploring how people from different cultures go about their lives. Although I was a complete geek at school and a swot throughout university, I loved socialising over great food and stories. As part of my four-year degree in English and Spanish, I lived in Madrid for a year, and whilst there, I perfected my Indian cooking in a different way. I lived next door to a Spanish restaurant and tapas bar and the staff became close friends. I would teach them English language skills through real-life cooking scenarios and entertaining. At the same time, teaching them how to cook Indian food connected me back to my family in London. During my short weekend trips to London, I would return to Madrid with a suitcase full of Indian herbs and spices. Entertaining my Spanish friends was great fun, and it united my passion for languages, food and socialising.

In recent years, a lot of people have talked and written about making Indian food 'healthy', presenting it as an unhealthy way of eating. I find it difficult to relate to this, as the Indian food that I've grown up on has always been cooked in a balanced style. Being health-conscious herself, whilst never afraid to indulge, my mum has always fed my sister, father and I Indian food which was nourishing, delicious and never swimming in oil! None of us are overweight, and we simply follow a balanced lifestyle, without a list of 'forbidden foods' or endless rules. I appreciate that Indian food can be cooked unhealthily, just as any cuisine can. My personal experience of Indian food is a positive one, based on eating well, and enjoying tasty dishes.

When my grandparents were growing up in India, information about 'healthy eating' was not readily available through the internet and social media. They had their own 'healthy' ways of cooking and eating that suited their particular lifestyles, budgets and tastes. I was surprised to learn from my dadima that her mother, my great-grandmother, would drink a cup of ghee (clarified butter) at 3am, in order to prepare her for a day of physical labour. I couldn't stop laughing when my dadima said: "Well, how else was she going to get the strength to do all that physical work?!" It makes perfect sense to me that eating carbohydrates and fats early on in the day would have given my great-grandmother a slow release of energy throughout the day – although 'modern' nutritionists would possibly frown at this.

I am really close to my dadima and I have spent a lot of time with her. Her philosophy is to eat everything in moderation, but stay active. The idea of going on a 'diet' has always seemed like a foreign concept to my family and I. I don't deny myself food, and resist following too many rules. If I feel like eating a couple of parathas for a weekend brunch, I will indulge. I'm just mindful of portion sizes, and lead an active lifestyle within my busy regime.

My mum also spent a lot of time with my dadima, her mother-in-law, as she lived in the extended family after marriage. Dadima's cooking habits rubbed off on her too, and as a result, she has raised my sister and I on mainly home-cooked Indian food. Growing up, I have seen my mum work long hours, and study

as part of a career in education. She always made time to cook for us, and put her 'superfood spin' on traditional Indian dishes wherever she could – using quinoa instead of rice, for example. The demands of juggling her career, and all the other roles that she played, meant that she would regularly batch cook and freeze healthy dishes to save time. As a result, it has become second nature for me to imitate her cooking approach. I've no doubt introduced some of her techniques into the recipes.

In this book, I make no apologies for not adding nutritional information alongside the recipes. This would be a fake approach for me to adopt, as none of the dadimas I have spoken to talk about food by measuring nutritional value. They take it for granted that they cook food that is 'good' for you, and the priority is delicious taste! If measuring nutritional values is your style, feel free to adapt the recipes with this in mind. Adjust recipes to suit your personal dietary requirements, lifestyle, and of course tastebuds!

Writing this book has led me to believe that the cooking experience improves with age, knowledge and life experience, particularly cooking for gatherings and large families. The dadimas that I have spoken to have all cooked for large family dinners and their hospitality is heart-warming. I was particularly drawn to the magical stories behind some of their dishes. Where dadimas have discussed special stories, I have included them in an effort to share that magic with you.

When I visit different countries on holiday, I love to sample the taste of their regional dishes. I do not think of the food alone, but rather, I am keen to learn about the culture and roots behind that dish or meal. Adventurous travellers will seek out restaurants and bars on side streets, away from the tourist traps – those hidden gems which serve authentic cuisine using tried and tested classic recipes.

To repeat my key message again, cooking is so much more than just creating food. I remember feeling amused by a Mexican book that I read at university, 'Como agua para chocolate' ('Like Water For Chocolate') by Laura Esquivel. At one point in the story, the feelings of the protagonist, who is madly in love, become so powerful. When she cooks and prepares for a dinner party, her emotions literally infuse the dishes. Through the act of eating her food, the guests experience her anger, passion and sadness. Although this may seem like a rather dramatic example (the story is of the magical realism genre), I love the simple message behind it. It reminds me of my grandparents' teachings – they always stress the importance of cooking with a loving and happy heart, as they believe that food will be all the tastier for it. They must be right, because whenever my nanima (mum's mother) cooked something and it was not to her usual high standards, my nanaji (mum's father) would shake his head in dismay, and tell her that she had cooked it with anger or stress on that particular day. My dadaji (grandad) always stresses to me that whatever you do in life, even if it's just sweeping a shop floor, do it with a happy heart and give it your full energy and passion.

Everyone will have their own little rituals when cooking, and I have many. When I am preparing food, I think carefully about the people I am cooking for and my desire for them to enjoy the food together over good conversation. When I'm entertaining, I need to be in a certain headspace so that I can juggle cooking a few dishes at a time and plan ahead with my preparation so that it's an enjoyable experience. I love cooking to Spanish reggaeton music, jazz, or anything with a strong rhythm, as it reminds me of my exciting student days in Madrid. I will put on my favourite apron, pour myself a nice cuppa, or even indulge in a small glass of wine and my favourite Kalamata olives. These small rituals help to create a positive cooking and entertaining mood in the kitchen, allowing me to relax and enjoy the cooking experience. Personally, I enjoy cooking alone, but do get your friends and family involved if that suits your style. Before you dive in, though, I have one small request. Use this book with your heart and soul, and experiment creatively. It doesn't matter if you leave grubby haldi fingerprints across the pages, or scribble your own special stories or recipe modifications next to mine. Your marks are important memories to you, and show how culinary wisdom travels and connects generations. I hope these stories and recipes are as enjoyable for you to cook as they were for me to learn, adapt and write. Thank you for buying my book, and in doing so, appreciating my effort to keep the legacies of 'ordinary', yet 'extraordinary', grandmothers alive.

Kitchen Wisdom

I've written this chapter to share some culinary tips that I've gathered from cooking the dishes in this book, as well as tips from observing my mum over the years. Kitchen Wisdom could be a book in itself, and this short chapter can only gloss over key areas. As I've stated in the introduction, I'm not a chef, but I am a passionate home cook. The pointers I share have certainly made my life easier when experimenting with the dadimas' recipes, and I hope they do the same for you. Don't feel under pressure to follow my tips, as these suit my lifestyle, approach to cooking, and cooking preferences. If you're fairly new to cooking South Asian cuisine, I hope they help to get you started. If you're already a pro, feel free to get stuck into cooking!

In this chapter I've focused on the essentials and tried not to overcomplicate matters. After all, most of the dadimas in this book learnt to cook from humble means. They used simple ingredients and tools to produce delicious meals.

There will be more kitchen wisdom tips from our fabulous dadimas, sprinkled throughout the book.

Measurements

One of the things I learnt from a young age, through observing my mum and dadima, is that delicious Indian cooking does not require obsessive measuring. When I used to make rotis with my dadima, I would ask her how much water to add to the flour. She would casually reply with: "You just know when it looks and feels like this." Whenever I quizzed my mum on how much of each spice to add to a dish, she would say: "Just gauge it from the colour, texture, taste and aroma," and her favourite phrase: "Just use your instinct and initiative!" The dadimas in this book learnt to cook through creative trial and error, and lots of practice and passion for feeding their families. By not being afraid to play around with quantities, they have the confidence to make instinctive judgements at speed, with real confidence. I gave up a long time ago asking about quantities, as that question was always greeted with a blank expression which said: "How long is a piece of string?!" It was only through watching the dadimas like a hawk that I worked out their individual cooking styles, and then understood how they used spices, before I started to re-create the dishes in my own kitchen.

My point is this: although I have given specific quantities in this book – it is a recipe book after all – the dadimas that I know do not measure out their spices as an exact science. Instead, everything seems to be so approximate. To build up a judgement for measurements, it's helpful to use the same spoon when measuring out spices. To clarify, my reference to 1 teaspoon is 1 metric teaspoon (5ml) (slightly more than a standard household spoon) and the same for a tablespoon. Most of the dadimas in this book keep the same spoon in their spice container so that they can judge just by looking. It's not the end of the world if half a teaspoon of extra garam masala goes into your dish, or a quarter of a teaspoon of paprika too little. With spices, I advise to start with smaller quantities, then you can always increase the amount the next time you cook the dish. Just relax, go with your gut instinct, and start building your own judgements over time, depending on your tastebuds.

Recipe titles and terms

I'm going to be using some Punjabi titles and terms in this book, and it might be a little different to the norm, but here's why I'm doing it. As synonymous as the words 'curry' and 'gravy' have become with Indian dishes and their saucy textures, I find that they don't necessarily describe the cooking philosophy of the dadimas in this book, and most of the dadimas I have met through this book journey. I have never grown up with dishes called 'curries', and was always surprised when people told me I should know what it was because I am Indian! I appreciate that we're all familiar with the word 'curry' in Britain (and oh how I adore our 'curry' culture!), but my dadima and nanima (grandmothers) certainly aren't familiar with 'curries'. As far as I know, there is only one North Indian dish which sounds remotely similar to the English word 'curry', and that's 'kadhi', a yoghurt-based dish that contains pakoras. The use of the word 'curry' to describe Indian cuisine has a fascinating history in its arrival to Britain. It makes sense to use 'curry' for language ease and speed, but in my view, it can also stereotype and exoticise Indian food under one heading.

I share recipes and techniques passed down through generations with our grandmothers. In sharing their wisdom, I'd like to do so through the familiar lens of each dadima, but also myself, in how I re-created their dishes. On those grounds, I could not justify the use of the word 'curry' in this particular context. Maybe it's four years of studying a language degree which has made me particularly pedantic about this subject!

Tharka

On the note of terminology, I'll be using the word 'tharka' a lot in my book. It's hard to find a direct English translation of this term but it's also known as a 'masala'. Some use the word to describe a technique, but my dadimas always use it to refer to the crucial mix of ingredients that serve as a base to many Indian dishes. Typically, it's a mixture of onions, ginger, garlic, spices and (sometimes) tomatoes, and the consistency varies in how dry or runny it is, based on the dish being cooked.

The dadimas that I have spoken to always told me (with raised eyebrows and a serious face) that a good tharka is the key to making a delicious dish. There's a knack to it, but once you master it through practice, it'll become second nature.

I cannot speak for all Indian dishes, but the dishes that you will read about in this book are inspired by Northern Indian cuisine, and the tharka pertaining to this region is generally not of a runny, gravy-like consistency.

Typical tharka mistakes are when it is overcooked or burnt, which happens when it is rushed or left unattended. The trick is to take your time – at this vital stage you really need to nurture all your ingredients over a moderate heat. Make sure that you have enough oil or ghee in your pan at the beginning, so that the onions can cook well, and the spices are protected from burning. If you're using turmeric powder, this usually goes in as one of the first spices so that it is cooked in well. If when you're cooking your tharka it starts to stick, you can add a splash of water, rather than more oil (specified in the recipes). Similarly, you can add a splash of water before adding spices as this protects them from burning. The secret to knowing when your tharka is done is when the oil separates from the tomatoes, forming little bubbles around the mixture. The consistency will thicken so that when you stir, it will feel as though it's moving together in one sweep. The dadimas in this book rarely leave their tharka unattended – towards the end, it needs regular stirring over a moderate heat to gauge when it's at a perfect texture.

Your tharkas will vary slightly across dishes, so my tip is, if you are freezing tharka, do so before the spices are added. This will offer you greater flexibility in your preparation of food. You'll find more tips on freezing and batch preparing overleaf.

Utensils

You'll see that I sometimes specify which cookware is preferred for certain dishes. This is because the dadimas believe it's really important to cook with the appropriate pan to get the optimum taste. This is not necessarily from a brand perspective, but rather for the shape and surface area of the utensils.

I know that nowadays many of us – me included – use non-stick kitchenware, which is great. However, a lot of the dadimas that I spent time with, my own dadimas included, also like using stainless steel karahis – the heavy-based, bowl-shaped Indian pans. These are particularly well-suited to meat and some vegetable dishes.

Although using a karahi requires more stirring to make sure nothing sticks to the base of the pan, this is all part of the rich flavour-infusing process. If a few onions stick to the bottom, that crispiness enriches the flavour – just make sure the onions don't burn. My dadimas all had karahis in their kitchen. The bowl-shaped base is thought to help food cook evenly, where the cooking oil pools at the bottom and coats your onions fully.

Spice container

I'd like to think that this book doesn't call for too many kitchen gadgets which you wouldn't otherwise keep at home. But if you do plan on cooking Indian food regularly, one thing I would recommend buying is a spice container. You can find them online, and they aren't too pricey. They are usually stainless steel, circular containers with seven little bowls which you can refill with your most-used spices. Your spice container will be your go-to kitchen container for most of the recipes in this book! If you can't get hold of one, use any compartmentalised container where you can store all your spices in one place.

Spices

The great thing about spice containers is that you can choose to fill them with whichever spices you want, depending on your own taste and preferences. Most of the dadimas that I interviewed had two containers: one for whole spices, and one for powdered ones. For the recipes in this book, I like to fill my spice container with the following powdered spices (I leave a few out as there are sadly only seven bowls!):

1. Haldi (turmeric powder)
2. Paprika
3. Salt
4. Ground black pepper
5. Garam masala (Some people make their own garam masala by selecting each individual whole spice; some of the dadimas in the book do this. Others buy pre-prepared bags of 'whole garam masala' whole spices, and grind that as they go. I like to do the latter – it's a nice compromise. Alternatively, you can buy powdered garam masala if that's more convenient)
6. Cumin seeds, whole
7. Red chilli powder (check the packet before buying. Kashmiri chillies are milder. I use standard red chilli powder in this book)
8. Coriander powder (dhania powder)

Whole spices:
Cinnamon shards
Brown cardamom (optional)
Green cardamom
Cloves

Oil and ghee

I always prefer to cook with rapeseed oil for Indian cooking, as it has a higher boiling point than olive oil, which we need for making a really good tharka. Always read the ingredients when buying oil – a lot of the time, vegetable oil is actually rapeseed oil.

Ghee (known as clarified butter because the milk solids are removed) is also used in some of the recipes in this book. It's a common alternative to oil in Indian cooking, and is my favourite natural fat. As well as its enticingly buttery aroma, its high boiling point makes it ideal for cooking ingredients. You can buy ghee (often called 'pure butter ghee') from supermarkets, but it is also really easy to make and store in an airtight container, as you would with butter. My dadima always makes her own, and here's how she does it.

Use 6 x 250g blocks of unsalted butter – this usually makes between 1.1-1.2kg of ghee for me (it

depends on the duration of boiling and the butter block). You can scale down the quantity as you wish. It keeps well in a clean, airtight container, refrigerated, for 2-3 months – but always check for obvious signs of spoilage or smell if unsure. In a heavy-based, non-stick saucepan, melt the butter blocks over a moderate heat. There's no need to stir initially, but as soon as the butter starts to melt, stir and bring to a gentle boil over a moderate heat so that it doesn't burn. Whilst it's boiling, you'll see a foamy layer. Once it's come to a good boil, the foam will start to disappear. Lower the heat to a simmer and stir the liquid part of the mixture regularly. The solid impurities will be settling at the bottom of the pan – they look like little rice grains. Don't scrape the bottom of the pan when you stir – we need to leave these impurities settled as they are. Simmer until the liquid runs clear. Test by using a spoon to regularly check that the liquid looks clear. Once it's done, drain the liquid through a fine sieve into the airtight container that you'll store it in. The sieve will collect the impurities as you pass the liquid through it. Leave to cool, then refrigerate. Spoon out the ghee as and when required – it will melt quickly once heated.

Some of the recipes in this book require shallow frying or deep frying – do re-use your fresh oil after the first use. I tend to store the cooled oil in a plastic container and reuse it once before disposing of it. Frying is not something I'd recommend for everyday cooking – it's more of a naughty treat every now and then. The oil quantity will depend on the size and shape of your pan, as well as the quantity of food being fried. However, for the recipes in this book which require shallow frying, I use an oil depth of around quarter of an inch in a wide frying pan, and for deep frying, I use a karahi and keep an oil depth of around 2-2.5 inches.

Planning and preparing

Here I want to share with you my most valuable tips for meal planning and preparing ahead. You'll also find 'prepare ahead' notes on the recipes where applicable. I promise you that by being organised (and making use of your trusted freezer), home cooking dadima-style food will be fun, efficient and something you can actually look forward to!

Getting the basic, repetitive tasks out of the way in advance, allows you to focus on the actual act of cooking. Lifestyles have become so busy, and although it would be lovely to enjoy home-cooked food from scratch every day, people just don't have the hours. These nuggets of wisdom have been passed down to me from the dadimas I have learnt from, but mostly from my superwoman mother who is the queen of juggling! The most important thing here is to ensure that your ingredients are all fresh to begin with, as then they'll freeze well.

Garlic and ginger

Some cookery books I've read recommend pre-making a batch of garlic and ginger paste. Whilst you can do this, I prefer to freeze my garlic and ginger separately as it offers me greater flexibility and control when it comes to cooking. Certain dishes need less of one and more of the other, so it's easier to blend the quantity you need just before cooking. I like to freeze garlic as whole cloves rather than blending it so that I have the option to crush/blend/grate or chop from frozen as required. With ginger, I peel it, roughly blend it in the food processor, and then freeze into small cubes (ice-cube trays are great for this) or small plastic containers.

Onions

Let's face it, nobody wants to be chopping these tear-jerkers every evening after work! But the fact is that onions are a staple ingredient in many Indian dishes. In some cases, it's much more efficient to prepare them all at once, rather than having that lingering onion smell. I appreciate that some of the dishes in this book call for freshly-cut onions (like pakoras), but for those dishes with a tharka, pre-cooked onions save you time at the first key step: softening the onions. Because different dishes call for different levels of browning the onions, I pre-cook my onions so that they've just softened – that way I have flexibility. When I lived alone in Cambridgeshire, I would blitz this job on a Sunday morning, giving myself a head start for a long work week ahead. Remember to close the kitchen door and open the windows!

What you need: 10 onions (white or red), rapeseed oil, cumin seeds (optional), and a blender. I always keep a supply of pre-cooked red and white onions in my freezer, as I prefer red in some of my meat dishes.

What to do: Peel and wash the onions, then roughly dice so that you can place them in the blender. Do not blitz them into a paste – we're after a cut which will serve a broad range of dishes. Aim for a chopped to finely chopped consistency. For greater flexibility, chop half of them, and slice the other half – that way you have two different cuts ready to use. Fry them at the same time, but in separate pans.

Heat enough oil to coat all the onions in a wide, non-stick pan. Do not scrimp on oil here – you need enough to brown the onions without burning them. Once the oil is hot, add a few teaspoons of cumin seeds (this is optional). When the seeds are sizzling, add your onions and stir over a medium heat until softened and light brown.

Once cooked, let your onions cool, then transfer into plastic containers. I always label and date my containers before placing them in the freezer. To use, just defrost them in the fridge the day before you want to cook with them, or even the same morning, and that gives you that little head start before cooking.

Green chillies

Add chillies to personal taste, and always check the spice factor before buying. Do bear in mind that every single chilli is different, even if it's the same type or from the same pack! I tend to use green finger chillies for the recipes in this book, but I use rocket chillies when cooking for my family, as they like a bit of a kick! Again, for flexibility, I like to freeze my chillies whole. That way, they can be thrown in whole, chopped or blended as necessary – they defrost quickly. However, if you prefer, blend them all at once and pop them into ice-cube trays.

Coriander

Fresh coriander is a commonly-used herb ingredient (and garnish) in Indian food. As such, washing, de-stalking and chopping this herb is another job that you don't always want, if you are cooking Indian food regularly.

Take a bunch of fresh coriander and strip the leaves from the stalks. Wash thoroughly and then leave to dry on a tea towel overnight (or for a few hours). Once fully dry, chop roughly and freeze in freezer bags or plastic containers. The great thing about frozen coriander is that because it is such a delicate herb, it defrosts immediately when you add it to a dish, so no need to take it out of the freezer in advance. Sometimes fresh coriander is preferred, such as when making mixtures for pakoras, aloo tikkis, or for garnishing food when you have guests over. Although fresh is great, I always keep a frozen back-up supply, and it saves any wastage.

Our dadimas were always taught by their own parents and grandparents to discard the tough coriander stalks, but if you are worried about food waste or simply like the taste, you can also add them – just make sure they are finely chopped.

Tinned tomatoes

It's always worth keeping tinned tomatoes in your store cupboard for Indian cooking. For the recipes in this book, I tend to specify tinned plum tomatoes or tomato passata. The dadimas in this book have their preferences, but if you have a tin of chopped tomatoes at home, and the recipe says plum tomatoes or passata, you don't have to worry about going out to buy them especially. The key with tomatoes is to cook them with the spices and onions until they reach the correct consistency of a 'tharka'.

Cook now, eat later

You'll notice that many of the recipes in this book serve a fair number of guests (and that's with me scaling them down). That's because all of the dadimas in this book, for various reasons, are used to cooking in large quantities so there's always extra for a few more guests. They've all entertained a lot in the past, and have had big families to feed. Nowadays, they often prepare extra for their children and grandchildren to take home with them to freeze, or refrigerate for a few days. Even those dadimas for whom freezing was once a foreign concept in India, seem to have come around to the benefits of cooking a little extra for a busy day.

I've written on each recipe where it's possible to freeze and maintain the taste, or save for another day. Equally, there are some dishes that are simply best enjoyed fresh on the day.

Indian ingredients

I'm fortunate to live close to Indian supermarkets, or large supermarkets with good 'world foods' aisles. I've tried to be specific within the recipes about Indian ingredients, and what name to look for when buying them. If you can, do make a trip to your local Indian supermarket, but if that's not possible, you can always buy Indian groceries online.

Entertaining

The recipes in this book are meant to be shared through some fun evenings of good conversation and entertainment – dadima's style is all about sharing!

The dadimas in this book are always mindful of complementary textures and flavours when preparing a meal, as well as which dishes are lighter or more filling. You might find the guide below useful if you're planning which dishes to prepare ahead for a feast with your friends or family. It's really hard to generalise, and it's by no means comprehensive – it's just a suggestion to help you narrow down the choices. If you're going for a more everyday meal then one or two dishes is plenty, accompanied with yoghurt and rice or chapattis. Many of the dishes are versatile in that they can be served as starters, main meals or snacks.

The suggested menu below is great if you want to impress your friends or family with a full meal:

1. A rice dish and/or rotis (chapattis)
2. A lentil dish or another wet dish with a sauce to it
3. A vegetable dish (which is known as a subji)
4. A meat or fish dish (if you eat meat)
5. A salad, to personal taste (optional)
6. Accompaniment: Plain natural yoghurt or raita yoghurt (bear in mind that yoghurt is not traditionally served with fish) or chutney

That's enough of my humble suggestions for now. As well as the kitchen wisdom tips sprinkled throughout the book, I really hope that you enjoy reading the life advice of each dadima along the way, as much as I enjoyed listening and learning from these talented women.

Santosh

mah di daal

aloo bhengan

aloo palak pakoras

masala chai

semiyan

Don't worry about expensive clothes - put your energy into good food, health and wellbeing.

antosh, my dadima, is one of the most influential and extraordinary women in my life. She is the inspiration behind dadima's. I have listened to her captivating stories ever since I was a little girl and have never tired of them. She would tell me stories all day – whilst walking me to school, colouring with me, or whilst she massaged oil into my hair and plaited it (her traditional beauty remedy). I would look forward to her telling me my favourite bedtime story, the Indian folktale *ik si chiri, te ik si kaan* (There was once a sparrow, and a crow). I memorised the tale, wide-eyed, questioning with such passion as to why the sparrow would not share a meal with her husband. My dadima, a professional storyteller (or so it seemed to me), would add a clever spin each time.

Santosh was born in the early 1940s, and spent her childhood and teen years in North-West India (the Punjab), in a city called Jalandhar. Although raised in India, Santosh was born into what is now called Pakistan since the partition of India in 1947. This was a historical period characterised by riots, bloodshed and upheaval. As a result, Santosh and her family fled their hometown when she was around five years of age to start a new life in the Punjab (in India). Thought to have been the largest mass migration in history, Santosh and her family were not alone in their journeys.

As one of 11 children, Santosh (affectionately called 'Toshi') spent much of her early girlhood lending a helping domestic hand to her mother. Having left all of their wealth and belongings behind, the family had to start from humble beginnings again. Seeing Santosh's selfless nature, her dad adored her as his princess. Santosh, not usually emotional, wells up a little whilst recalling how her dad would put together a tea party for he and his favourite daughter, in their modest kitchen. On a weekly basis, he would come home after work and lay the table with their best cloth and crockery, set out a cushion for young Santosh, and sit on the floor himself. Whilst the other siblings would enquire if they were having guests over, young Santosh would smile shyly at her dad's gesture. She remembers how she walked miles to collect pails of water from the well, washed laundry by hand, and did what she enjoyed most: watch her mother cook. What she desired above all else was to cook a dish as appetising as her mother's. She refers to this as 'khan vale dah dil khushi hoye' – loosely translated as 'to cook so well that it warms the heart of the diner'.

Santosh's mother taught her how to make the essential dishes which she still makes today; rotis (chapattis) and parathas (stuffed flatbread). It was her dadaji (grandfather) who taught young Toshi how to make her favourite bread, 'makki di roti' (chapatti made with cornmeal, traditionally enjoyed with saag), when she was only seven years old.

At the age of 16, Santosh's cooking repertoire grew to include mouth-watering meat, fish, lentils, subjis (vegetable dishes) and puddings, all thanks to her arranged marriage. Her cooking teachers were no longer her mother or dadaji, but instead her mother-in-law. This is when she learnt the art of improvisation and following one's instincts.

After ten days of settling into her new marital home, Santosh's culinary skills were put to the test when her father-in-law requested karah (a sweet dish with sacred significance – see Indu's recipe on p173) to be served to the family. This was an auspicious ritual for a new bride. Young Santosh had eaten karah several times, but had never made it. Santosh had to rely on her instincts and imagination, and that must have done the trick: her father-in-law praised her cooking for being as good as his wife's, and announced that from that point forward, she was to cook for the family. No pressure!

What she was to cook, though, was a daily surprise. Sat on the floor, using whatever ingredients her mother-in-law bought from the local markets, Santosh would heat up the 'chulha' (traditional Indian indoor cooking stove) and experiment with karele (bitter gourd), aloo bhengan (potato and aubergine in masala), different lentils, meats and fish. Raised as a pure vegetarian, 16-year-old Santosh was bewildered when her mother-in-law placed in front of her the head of a goat to prepare with dinner. Her mother-in-law showed her the technique of skinning the head, and then left her to continue!

Santosh attributes her fast learning skills to the fact that she was young, naive, and keen to please her new family. "That's why they used to get girls married so young," she says, "so they could adapt before they were old enough to understand and question too much."

In 1965, aged 22 and a mother to her first two children, Santosh was about to face new hurdles with her move to the UK. My dadaji (grandfather), Kasturi, had been working in the UK, and when he secured permanent residency, he wanted his wife and children to live with him. Nomadic room-renting in West London characterised the next year or so of Santosh's life.

Moving into their first home did not take long, as Kasturi rented a room for the four of them in the house of an Indian family in West London. They didn't have much money and rent was just about affordable: £4 a week. With a £10 weekly salary, £6 went towards feeding the family for the week.

Santosh's first landlady insisted that no pots, pans or cutlery could be left in the kitchen, and that one of the conditions of tenancy was to clean the entire house and to be limited to a 30-minute kitchen slot to prepare food. This bizarre treatment wasn't unique: the next landlords told Santosh she could only enter the house from the back gate and must not breathe a word of her family's residency to anyone. My dadima lived almost in secret.

On one occasion, Santosh was in her room with her children, just about to eat dinner, when she was summoned to the kitchen as the cooker had supposedly not been thoroughly cleaned! Today Santosh is forgiving and philosophical about it all: "'It wasn't like we had to make a lot of subjia (vegetable dishes)," she says. "If you're in someone else's kitchen you don't want to spend long in there anyway."

Back then, Santosh didn't have all day to cook dinner and take pleasure in what she was creating – she was cooking purely out of necessity. In India she used to make everything, from spiced courgettes to masala turnips, cholay (chickpeas) to kheer (rice pudding), but in the UK she would cook fast and simple food to satisfy her husband's hunger after a long shift at work. She would prepare parathas, rotis, different daal dishes, cholay and partha (aubergines). She would also make her husband (and his work friends) a few parathas for breakfast, filled with subji (vegetable dish) and cheese, and sent them off with a flask of masala chai. She cooked plentifully for all!

Whilst times were hard, Santosh cared only for the future of her precious children. Of course she missed her home in India, where she was adored like a princess by her parents, where she would visit the local shops and markets, and socialise with people. In England, she had no friends, her husband was at work from 5am, she was house-bound for childcare, and could hardly even contact her family – the cost of one phone call was too expensive and a letter could take weeks to arrive. All she had were her memories and her children, and she treasured them. Trying to cope with the upheaval of settling in England, she must have experienced what we now class as depression, though it had no title then. Any sad feelings were fought off for the sake of her children.

In due course, my dadaji saved enough money to put down a deposit for his first property, a three-bedroom house for £4,500. In this and subsequent houses that they moved to, Santosh raised the rest of her children, and also hosted her mother-in-law on four or five occasions. Santosh's mother-in-law was a tough woman, and rarely praised her for her hard work. But when visiting the UK, she soon realised how capable Santosh was at running a house, raising six children and being a dutiful wife – and finally gave her the praise she deserved!

Today, through her six doting children, Santosh is grandmother and great-grandmother to many children. She is the calmest and most gentle woman in the family, and the ultimate feeder. Nothing delights her more than seeing her children and grandchildren, cooking for her family, and seeing them enjoy her food. Even after wowing everyone with her culinary skills, her humble motto of 'nothing is hard to cook' makes me beam with adoration to this day. I love sitting at my dadima's kitchen table, eagerly waiting for my hot paratha, whilst remembering that this was the very same room in which I celebrated my first four birthdays.

Santosh is the family philosopher, always on hand to offer her words of wisdom. When looking for a life partner, she stresses the importance of finding a 'good' man (she refers to a man, as it is me she is advising).

She describes a 'good man' as someone who has a pure heart, is understanding, faithful and respectful to his wife, and also respectful of his elders. Money isn't the most important thing – if he has potential, skills and works hard, money can be made gradually to support a family and the rest will fall into place. If a man does not have a good work ethic or lies, Santosh advises to steer clear! Know the difference between true love, which is long-lasting, takes work and survives both sorrows and joys, and the love which lasts for only two minutes.

When it comes to money, Santosh believes that one should never scrimp on health and food. She thinks that you should invest time and energy in good food, your health and wellbeing, and what makes you really happy, rather than worrying about expensive material possessions.

Santosh is obsessed by small details, and this obsession translates into cleanliness and perfectionism in cooking. She will scrub a steel tea pot until you can see your face in it, sift through raw lentils like a hawk, and cut and cook her onions until they are really small and soft – she worries about the larger ones getting stuck in the throat. My dadima is also precious about her tharka (the masala base – see Kitchen Wisdom). She stands by her tharka stirring, and tells me of hypothetical scenarios where it could burn if left unattended, and how it would be unappetising for any guest to eat should that happen. This is also the case for other dishes – she stands by her stove until she's certain it's ready for simmering. I too have therefore picked up this habit!

I, along with her other grandchildren, appreciate and love dadima's little quirks, particularly her fussy approach in choosing only the finest ingredients – she will pick up and inspect each and every vegetable before buying it. She is a naturally resourceful cook – she grinds her own spices for garam masala and masala chai, and ensures no leftover ginger goes to waste by using it to make ginger tea. If there's one message I've taken away from shopping and cooking with my grandmother over the years, it's how important fresh food and good home-cooking is for a healthy mind, body and soul. As she said to me recently: "New clothes, make-up and shoes will come and go, but you have one body for life, and you must look after it." My precious dadima – so wise, so loving!

Santosh cooks such a wide array of dishes that it was difficult to pick and choose for this book (as was the case for the each of the other dadimas). I've cherry-picked my ultimate favourites, and the ones I know she secretly loves to cook.

Mah di daal
(Black urad lentils)

It's safe to say that of all of my dadima's beautiful recipes, mah di daal is her signature dish. Mah di daal (mother's daal) is the familiar name for this classic dish from the Punjab, where Santosh was raised. Santosh keeps her recipe and method close to her chest, and rightly so! She innocently makes the dish before anyone arrives (she even tried this with me and I'm her granddaughter!). It happens to be one of my favourite dishes of all time — it tastes like home.

Everyone in my family melts at the thought of dadima's wholesome, heartwarming daal. Knowing that her sons and daughters will swing by as soon as they hear she's making it, Santosh makes a huge pot of it in anticipation. My mum always tells me that there is a real art to making this daal, and having cooked it, I would agree.

In India, my dadima would have this daal simmering for a good 24 hours, and this was what made it so flavoursome. When she entertained a lot, she would still do this in the UK. Nowadays she uses a pressure cooker, and it tastes equally divine. Santosh's secret to preserving that slow-cooked flavour is to simmer the daal both before and after pressure cooking, so that there is no compromise on taste. Santosh advises that the longer you can leave it to simmer gently, the tastier it is. It's also really important that your tharka is flavoured well.

It goes without saying, but do take the relevant safety precautions when using a pressure cooker. My preferred method of releasing the pressure is to allow it to release naturally by leaving it in a sink and pouring cold water over the top.

This daal is so rich and naturally flavoursome that it asks of a subtle pairing such as jeera rice or plain rice, or a few rotis and a bowl of yoghurt. You can serve it with most dishes, but for variety in texture and taste, try and opt for a dry meat dish or subji (vegetable dish). If you fancy tweaking this dish, add kidney beans during cooking — this is something Santosh often does. However, her classic dish is pure and simple urad lentils and that's the recipe you'll find below.

Serves 5-6
For the daal:
 250g black daal (sold as whole urid/urad lentils in Indian supermarkets)
1 teaspoon salt (or to taste)
1 level teaspoon turmeric powder
1.3-1.5 litres of water

For the tharka (onion masala base):
2 heaped tablespoons solid ghee (or 4 tablespoons rapeseed oil)
1 small onion, finely chopped
20g fresh ginger, peeled
4 garlic cloves
1 and a half teaspoons garam masala
1 heaped teaspoon coriander powder
Three quarter teaspoon black pepper

2 green finger chillies, blended (or to taste)
Half teaspoon paprika
Half teaspoon salt (or to taste) (already added to lentils)
200g tomato passata (or blended plum tomatoes)
Handful fresh finely chopped coriander leaves, to garnish

Recipe continued overleaf.

Mah di daal (continued)

1. Check the lentils and remove any stones or grit.

2. Wash the lentils thoroughly.

3. Put the lentils into a pressure cooker and fill with water. I prefer to add approximately 1.5 litres and cook off any excess water. Heat over a moderate flame without the pressure cooker lid. When the water is tepid add the salt and turmeric powder.

4. Bring to a gentle boil. Stir once in between so that the turmeric infuses and nothing sticks to the bottom of the pan.

5. Once the turmeric has boiled once with the lentils, pressure cook over a moderate heat until the lentils are soft to the touch. (If the heat is too high or there is not enough water, the daal can burn at the bottom of the pan.) This particular daal (lentil) takes a longer time to break down than other daals. The time will depend on your cooker – I pressure cook for around 45 minutes. After the first few whistles, I turn down the heat to a simmer, before letting it whistle another few times.

6. Allow the pressure to release (I do this in the sink) before opening the lid of the pressure cooker. Stir and check whether the lentils have softened. If there is still some excess water, don't worry – you can cook that off during simmering. The key is that the lentils are cooked.

7. Simmer in the pressure cooker without the lid on and stir occasionally.

8. In the meantime, take a separate pan to make your tharka. Gently heat the ghee or oil. My dadima always uses ghee for that extra creaminess. Don't scrimp on the oil or ghee here – there needs to be enough for the onions to cook through.

9. Add the onions and stir regularly until light brown.

10. Add ginger and allow to brown, stirring occasionally.

11. Add garlic and green chillies and stir.

12. Add around 40-45ml of water and then add the spices. Stir well over a moderate heat until the onions have shrunk a little and softened. Santosh always adds water as she believes it helps to bring out the flavour of the onions, whilst softening them and protecting the spices.

13. Add the tomatoes and mix well over a moderate-high heat. Cook until the tharka is done, stirring regularly. This is when oil bubbles form around the mixture and the consistency thickens.

14. Carefully pour the tharka into the lentils (or vice versa depending on the size of your pan).

15. Simmer the daal for 20 minutes until it's a medium consistency, stirring once or twice. Add boiling water if you prefer a runnier consistency.

16. Garnish with coriander, a cheeky dollop of ghee and serve hot.

Freeze note: For best results, thaw and re-heat the daal in a saucepan, adding a little boiling water to loosen the consistency.

Aloo bhengan
(Potatoes & aubergines)

The key to my dadima's aloo bhengan, soft enough to slice with a teaspoon, is to cover and simmer the potatoes (aloo) and bhengan (aubergines) gently in their tharka. She believes that the beauty of aloo bhengan is to enhance the natural flavour of the two key ingredients, and that simmering brings out a subtle smoky undertone to the dish, whilst softening to the point that the aubergines gently cling to the potatoes.

For my dadima, allowing the aubergines and potatoes to cook in their own steam is essential. I'll share her endearing steaming technique with you, so you can appreciate just how important this is to her. She's always placed a stainless steel plate on her pan (which is chosen to fit perfectly) on which she puts a large saucepan of water. Even though my dadima has lids for her saucepans, she hasn't shaken off the humble techniques she used in India as a young girl. I personally use a very well-fitted lid, as this can achieve the same results as my dadima's technique.

A foolproof tip from my dadima for evenly cooked aloo bhengan, is to always use a wide-based pan. I have my own favourite one. Santosh also likes to cook this dish using the long, slim baby aubergines. If using these, cook them whole, but create an opening by slicing each one into quarters, and not taking the knife right through the top of the aubergines. The aubergine needs to remain as one piece.

I like to eat aloo bhengan with fluffy rice (see Arun's rice on p122) or a few rotis and a generous serving of yoghurt.

Serves 4-5 as a side dish
5 tablespoons rapeseed oil
1 small onion, finely chopped
4 cloves garlic, peeled and blended
25g ginger, peeled and blended with the garlic
1 and a half teaspoons turmeric powder

Quarter teaspoon red chilli powder
2 green finger chillies, finely chopped (or to taste)
Half teaspoon paprika
1 level teaspoon black pepper
1 teaspoon salt
200g tomato passata
300g white medium-sized potatoes,

peeled and chopped into small chunks
1 aubergine (around 300g) (or baby aubergines, left whole but sliced almost to the top into quarters)
1 teaspoon garam masala
Fresh coriander, to garnish

1. Heat the oil and add the onions, stirring over a moderate heat for 2 minutes, before adding the garlic and ginger. Cook until the ingredients turn light brown.

2. Add around 50-60ml of water and stir over a moderate heat. This is Santosh's preferred method of softening the onions and protecting the spices. We're adding more than just a splash of water as it's needed to cook the potatoes. If there's not enough water, the potatoes will stick to the pan during simmering.

3. Add all the spices and green chillies, except for garam masala. Cook and stir regularly for 2 minutes.

4. Add the tomatoes and stir over a medium heat until your tharka is done. This is when the oil separates from the tomatoes as little bubbles around the mixture. Don't cook off the excess water – we need it for the potatoes.

5. Add the potatoes and aubergines. Fold into the tharka. Make sure that each piece is coated so that the flavour can infuse during simmering.

6. Check there's enough liquid in the pan before simmering. There should be plenty of tharka; enough to coat the aubergines and potatoes plus a little excess. If it's looking a little dry, add some boiling water (around 40-50ml) and stir.

7. Lower the heat to a simmer. Cover over with a tight-fitting lid and simmer for 30 minutes, or until the potatoes and aubergines have softened nicely, without being soggy. Make sure you do a regular check and stir to prevent any sticking (I usually check after 5-7 minutes, and then once more after that). Add a little boiling water if needed throughout this process.

8. Add the garam masala and stir through. Then garnish with coriander and serve hot.

Aloo palak pakoras
(Potato and spinach bhajis)

My dadima's pakoras (also known as bhajis) have long marked family celebrations and happy gatherings. There are many filling options for pakoras, but my dadima's favourite is the aloo (potato) and palak (spinach) one. Pakoras are the perfect starters, to be enjoyed in good company. If my dadima wants to go all out on her starter course, she'll also serve samosas, and barfi for a little sweetness. She serves pakoras with chutney, and insists that they should also be accompanied with a mug of masala chai to help digestion. I think the real reason is that she loves the warm and cosy association of chit-chat over chai and pakoras. There is an old Indian saying that pakoras are particularly tasty on a rainy day!

Santosh is pedantic about her flavoursome pakoras. Her trick to perfecting the taste every time is simple: prepare the ingredients with care, and always taste the first pakora before frying the rest of the batch. The beauty of doing this is that you can add extra ingredients or spices to your batter according to your own preferences, no problem. For Santosh, the cut of the ingredients is really important so that they add texture and shape to the pakoras – she likes her onions and potatoes sliced. Santosh also believes that the batter to pakoras is the make or break, literally. Some people make the batter alongside mixing the ingredients, but she always prefers to make the batter separately. Her secret is to take time to check that the batter is perfect before frying. She keeps it thick at first, so that it's balanced out when the other ingredients release their own water.

Santosh always grinds her own garam masala from whole spices. If you have a spice grinder and have the time, I'd recommend doing the same (see Kitchen Wisdom). If not, use a ready ground mix.

Pakoras taste best hot and freshly fried, accompanied with mint chutney (p160) , or imlee (tamarind) chutney (p176), or a squirt of ketchup. If you're entertaining and want the convenience, however, you can fry them prior to guests arriving and then heat them in the oven to serve.

Other than enjoying pakoras by themselves, they are also enjoyed in a quintessentially traditional dish called kadhi (see Kamla's classic kadhi recipe on p200) — you must try it. The great thing is is that any leftover pakoras can be put to good use in Kamla's recipe.

Serves 5-6
2 medium-sized white potatoes (around 400g)
1 white onion
250g gram flour (known as besan in some Indian supermarkets)
80-100ml water
30g fresh ginger, peeled
Green finger chillies to taste (I use

two), or half teaspoon red chilli powder
1 tablespoon freshly squeezed lemon juice (this makes them nice and crispy)
Handful freshly chopped coriander
150g spinach, roughly chopped
Oil, for deep frying

Spices:
2 and a half teaspoons salt (or to taste)
1 level teaspoon pomegranate powder (anardana)
Half teaspoon black pepper
1 teaspoon garam masala
Half teaspoon coriander seeds
Half teaspoon cumin seeds

Recipe continued overleaf.

Aloo palak pakoras (continued)

Preparation:

1. Peel and slice the potatoes fairly thinly and small – so that they will cook through when fried. I like to quarter them and then slice to around 4cm by 2cm pieces.
2. Slice the onions thinly and small – a similar size to the potato slices. However you cut the potatoes and onions will influence the shape of your pakoras.
3. Dry roast the coriander seeds and cumin seeds in a frying pan until fragrant and then grind to a powder in a pestle and mortar – this is worth it for the distinctive warmth it will add. It should equate to around two teaspoons of powder. Set aside.
4. Pour out oil for deep frying (don't heat just yet) and line a plate with two pieces of kitchen roll.

Making the pakoras:

5. Sift the gram flour into a large mixing bowl. Gradually add water, mixing with your hand to form a smooth and thick batter. To be safe, make the mixture on the thicker side and don't over handle it. It should fall leisurely from a spoon and be thick enough to coat the back of a spoon. Water is your best friend or enemy with this batter – flexibility and judgement is required. We have yet to add ingredients, which will release their own water (varying depending on whether you have just washed them and individual water content). You can add a little more water/gram flour later if necessary.
6. Heat oil for deep frying. In the meantime, add the potatoes, spinach, ginger, green chillies, lemon juice, and spices to the mixing bowl. Mix well so that the ingredients are evenly spread. Taste a lick of the mixture at this point. Add more spices according to preference.
7. Test the consistency of the batter now that all ingredients have been added. If the batter was on the thick side earlier, it should have balanced out now to a medium consistency batter. All ingredients should be coated. Bear in mind the ingredients will release more water with time so if it looks thin, sift in some more gram flour and stir. It's important to have enough gram flour, or else the mixture can come apart in the oil.
8. Test that the oil is hot enough for frying; drop in a tiny ball of the batter and check that it rises. Keep the heat on medium. It's really important that this heat is maintained constantly throughout the frying process – it will make the pakoras golden and cooked through evenly without burning. If the oil is not hot enough, oil will soak into the pakoras.
9. Scoop up a handful of the batter using your hands. To prepare dadima's style of pakora, make sure each scoop has a slice of potato along with the spinach and onions. Keep the batter close to the tips of your fingers so it's easy to drop into the oil. Carefully push the pakora batter from your fingertips into the oil using your thumb. If you're new to this, try putting the batter onto a tablespoon and pushing it from there into the oil – just don't let the spoon touch the oil.
10. Fry the pakoras in batches until crisp and golden brown, over a medium heat. Leave a little space between each pakora so that they don't join together. Don't stir them initially, but after a minute do give them a stir and turn once or twice during cooking. Use a slotted spoon to drain off excess oil and transfer onto your lined plate.
11. This part is important: pause and taste this first pakora for salt and chilli. This is your chance to add more spices to the batter if required. If you do so, make sure you mix well afterwards.
12. Repeat steps 9 to 10 to make the remaining pakoras. If at any point you find that there are not enough potatoes or spinach per pakora, just add a bit more to the batter. It's worth doing this so you don't compromise on taste!
13. Serve fresh and hot with masala chai.

Freeze note: Once cool, you can freeze any leftover pakoras (if there are any!) and they keep well for a month. You can use them to make Kamla's kadhi on another occasion. If you're not freezing them, store in a cool dry place to eat any leftovers the next day (I'd recommend a pakora sandwich if you're stuck for options).

Masala chai

If you like warming spices and a hug in a mug, then this tea is for you. My dadima religiously starts her day with a mug of masala chai and enjoys it as an afternoon cuppa, just as the British do. Masala chai can be made from different spice combinations depending on individual family tastes. My dadima calls it saunf chai (fennel tea) and that's the familiar name I've grown up with too.

It just so happens that the spices which form the base to this tea, including fennel, cardamom, cloves, black peppercorns, ginger and cinnamon, are great for digestion. In the interest of appreciating one key flavour, my dadima believes that one should choose a few spices rather than throwing them all in. But she is also a strong advocate of 'each to their own'. For her own ayurvedic reasons, Santosh has two favourite combinations. She calls these her 'winter brew' and her 'everyday brew' (translated). It was after a few avoidance antics, which became a running joke in the family, that she shared those recipes with me. Her winter brew is perfect for when you're feeling a little run down or need something to warm you up from the inside. It contains cinnamon, black cardamom, cloves and black peppercorns. Her everyday brew contains fennel seeds (saunf), green cardamom and a little cinnamon.

As well as preferred spices, there are also different techniques to making this all-time classic; some people grind their whole spices into a powder, whilst others like to crush them whole with a pestle and mortar. For example, I enjoy chai once or twice a week as a novelty, so I enjoy the ritual of picking my cardamoms and the sound of them being crushed in a pestle and mortar. Because my dadima enjoys chai on a daily basis and believes the flavours are released better through grinding, she prefers the first option. My dadima grinds fennel seeds and green cardamoms in a spice grinder and pops that mixture into an airtight container for the week ahead. In a separate jar, she stores freshly ground cinnamon sticks. The ground mixture is more intense and concentrated than spices crushed using a pestle and mortar, so you don't need to use a lot of it.

My dadima always uses full fat milk to make her chai – as much as I tell her otherwise, she believes that anything with less fat is of a lesser quality.

My mum and dad had an introduced marriage. My dadima prepared her delicious brew of chai to welcome my mum's side of the family to her son's house on their first visit. Mum, 19 at the time, didn't go to this first visit as it was just for a few family members to meet. When my mum's aunty came back and reported to my mum, she said: "If you decide to marry that man, my child, the first thing you need to do is learn how to make chai from your mother-in-law!" To this day, my mum's side of the family still praise my dadima's famous masala chai.

If you're anything like me, you'll find it addictive, and have those days where you crave a mug of masala chai. There are a lot of masala tea bags available nowadays in shops and cafes, but for me the taste never matches a homemade brew.

You will need: a tea strainer, a spice grinder (for best results) or a pestle and mortar

See the masala chai recipe overleaf.

Masala chai (continued)

Everyday ground mix (makes 25-30 mugs depending on size and stores in an airtight container in a cool, dry place for a good two months):

20 green cardamom pods
2 teaspoons fennel seeds
Cinnamon stick, either a few small sticks or one large (mine is 7cm length by 2cm width)

1. Briefly crush the green cardamoms in a pestle and mortar to crack them open. Blitz to a powder with the fennel seeds in a spice grinder (shells and all). Empty into a container and pick out any shells left.
2. In a separate batch, crush the cinnamon sticks in a pestle and mortar so that they are small and then blitz to a powder in a spice grinder. Transfer to a separate container.

Winter warmer brew (makes 20-25 mugs depending on size of mugs. Storage as above):

3 small sticks of cinnamon, or 1 medium (mine are around 2cm length each)

8 cloves
2 black peppercorns
4 brown cardamoms

1. Briefly crush the brown cardamoms, to crack them open, along with cinnamon in a pestle and mortar. Then blitz to a powder along with the remaining spices in a spice grinder. Transfer to a separate container.

For the brew (makes 4 standard sized mugs):
1 mug milk (or to personal preference)
4 mugs cold water
Ground spices (for everyday brew; three quarter teaspoon fennel and green cardamom plus quarter teaspoon cinnamon. For winter brew: three quarter teaspoon)
Brown sugar or honey, to taste
3 teabags (For one person, use 1 teabag, but as a general rule of thumb, use one less teabag than the number of servings)

1. Pour the water into a large saucepan.
2. Heat the water and when tepid, add spices.
3. Bring to the boil and then add teabags.
4. Reduce the heat slightly and brew the teabags for 3-4 minutes.
5. Add milk. The brew should look milky – this balances out the intensity of the spices.
6. Turn up the heat and bring to the boil. Stand close by for this stage, as the milk can easily boil over the pan.
7. Wait for the milk to froth up and start to rise. Reduce the heat to a simmer to prevent it from boiling over. Getting your timings right here can be quite fun! The aroma of masala tea will be in its full glory now.
8. Simmer for a further 4-5 minutes and then bring to the boil a second time as in stage 7.
9. Squeeze and remove the teabags.
10. Over the sink, carefully pour the chai through a tea strainer into a teapot (when you pour into a teapot, you are less likely to get residue around the rim of the cup when serving).
11. Through a tea strainer again, just in case you missed any bits, pour the tea from the teapot at a height (to get that 'long pour') and add sweetness to taste. Enjoy hot.

Semiyan
(Sweet vermicelli milk pudding)

There are different words for this sweet vermicelli milk pudding. Being Punjabi, my dadima calls it semiyan (pronounced semi-yaa). It's a warming, satisfying and fragrant dessert, and one which I would always enjoy freshly cooked with my dadima, spooned straight from her steaming hot saucepan to my bowl. Semiyan are widely enjoyed at festivals and celebrations. That said, my dadima and my dadaji (grandfather) remember semiyan as a light dish they enjoyed in India whenever it took their fancy – they never needed a special occasion.

Nowadays vermicelli is available readymade, as are most pastas, but making fresh vermicelli was the only option available to my dadima in India, so she saw this as the norm. Semiyan is one of my grandfather's all-time favourite desserts, and he has vivid memories of exactly how it was made in India. It's no surprise, then, that he pottered around the kitchen whilst my dadima was showing me how she cooks it. Shushing each other and talking over one another, my grandparents reminisced about the women of their village patiently carrying out the cooking ritual (my dadima included) – and it was always the women, as the men would go out to work all day. They would start by making a thick semolina-based dough, then rolling it into a peda (dough ball). This dough would be fed through a machine which formed fine noodle-like strands, which were then collected and hung to dry outside before cooking. My dadaji said that before the machines were introduced, and even after they were, some of the elder women would mould the semiyan between their thumb and index finger. Santosh told me she and her fellow villagers were poor and never thought twice about how much effort it took to make something from scratch – they had no other choice. In fact, dadima was encouraged to be resourceful and learn how to make everything from scratch – from clothes and cooking to natural healing remedies. She thinks it's great that we have readymade things now, and looking back it may have been a lot of work doing things by hand, but she never worried that too much chopping and stirring would hurt her arms and so on.

Following the example of her mother and grandmother in India, my dadima's secret to semiyan is patience and gentle cooking – and always in ghee! It's really important to keep the heat low when cooking the vermicelli initially, so it doesn't burn. The only points where we need to turn up the heat are when the milk is added and when we're thickening the pudding. My dadima's tip is to always pre-boil the milk before adding it to the vermicelli, and to stir regularly.

Semiyan is really easy to tweak to your personal preference, adding dried fruits or crushed nuts to zhoosh it up and add extra warmth. My dadima's version is spiced with the seeds of green cardamoms, which she prefers to leave whole, and a few crushed nuts – she doesn't like to add lots of sugar, but you can adjust this to your taste. I personally prefer my dadima's semiyan with a few cloves, raisins and crushed pistachios. You can also add a cinnamon stick during cooking, removing once cooked. Semiyan is best enjoyed fresh, but if you do have any left over it can keep in the fridge for a day or two. It's perfectly normal for the semiyan to thicken and bundle together as they cool. To recreate the original consistency when re-heating, my dadima boils a little milk and adds the refrigerated semiyan to that. When freshly cooked, my dadima likes a medium-thick consistency which is pourable and easy to stir. The more milk you add, the runnier it is, and vice versa. It's difficult to judge the exact amount of milk, so another tip from my dadima is to boil a mug or so of extra milk just in case you feel like making the sauce thinner.

See the semiyan recipe overleaf.

Semiyan (continued)

Serves 4-5
1.4 litres full fat milk
2 and a half tablespoons solid ghee
(or unsalted butter)
100g broken vermicelli or whole
vermicelli
2 cloves
30g sultanas or raisins (optional)

Seeds of 8 green cardamoms (crush
open cardamom with a pestle and
mortar, remove seeds whole and
discard pods)
80g white sugar (or to taste)
1 level tablespoon crushed pistachios,
shells removed

1. Pour the milk into a saucepan and bring to the boil over a moderate heat. Try and use a heavy-based saucepan so that the milk doesn't burn at the bottom of the pan. Stir occasionally and switch off once it starts to froth up.

2. In a separate saucepan, melt the ghee or butter over a gentle heat. Add the vermicelli and stir, making sure it's all coated in ghee. If using whole vermicelli, use your spoon to break it up into small pieces in the saucepan.

3. Stir constantly over a gentle heat, lightly cooking and tossing the vermicelli until it's a toasted glazed golden brown (not dark brown). Santosh says that heating the vermicelli at this stage is important so that they cook thoroughly.

4. Stir in the cloves, raisins (if using) and cardamom seeds.

5. Take the saucepan off the heat. Carefully pour the boiled milk into the vermicelli, leaving around 200ml behind in case it's needed later.

6. Return to a low heat and stir, separating the strands of vermicelli. Then add the sugar and stir again.

7. Bring to the boil until it froths up, then simmer on a very low heat for 10 minutes, stirring once or twice in between to make sure nothing sticks to the bottom. At this stage you should see tiny heat bubbles on a still surface, along with a thin layer of ghee.

8. Give it a stir – you should feel that the sauce has thickened and the vermicelli has absorbed a lot of the milk. If you prefer a thinner consistency, add the remaining part of your boiled milk and simmer for a few minutes. (If you don't use the milk at this stage, keep it to make a delicious masala chai.) Bear in mind that your sauce will thicken as it cools, so it's advisable to make it a tad runnier than you'd like.

9. Stir in the crushed pistachios. Leave to sit, covered, for 5 minutes, before serving hot – it will thicken even more.

Bholi

rajma
aloo and mozzarella tikkis
pea and potato samosas
khoya
gorgeous gajrela
mango kulfi
almond and pistachio barfi

Your mother is your true best friend – she will always have your best interests at heart.

holi' (pronounced Polly) means innocent and gentle in Hindi, and is the affectionate nickname given to this dadima by her nearest and dearest. Bholi found it funny when I told her I was going to use her nickname over her first name, but it was really important that I familiarise you with her character as best I can. Another nickname is one given to her by her nine-year-old granddaughter, who has called her 'Gorgeous' since she was a toddler, and with adorable conviction at that.

Bholi was born in 1952 in India. Growing up as the third eldest of seven, Bholi spoke proudly about having a really special bond with her father. Her dad had a good job in sales and worked long hours to make ends meet, while her mum was a full-time homemaker. Aged four, and adamant that she would contribute to her dad's lunch, Bholi would eagerly assist her mum in the preparation of rotis (chapattis). She recalls how her dad would lovingly tell her how tasty her baby rotis were, despite them being as hard and dry as papadums!

In 1963, aged 11, Bholi moved to the UK from India with her family. Bholi's first week in the UK was spent in Birmingham, followed by a four-month stint at her nanaji's (grandfather's) home in Nottingham. It was a big five-bedroom house, but there was no central heating, carpets or bath, and the toilet was located in the back garden. Bholi remembers a cold winter period when the outdoor pipes froze, and her uncles would pour hot water over the pipes to get them working again. Bholi's mum would take her children to the public baths and bathe them there instead. After four months in the UK, her dad had saved enough money to put down a deposit for a two-bedroom house for £1,000 in Nottingham. To her delight, this house did have a bathroom!

In the meantime, Bholi began her school life in Nottingham. She was a clever girl at school, but with her limited English language skills, she struggled to keep up. Fortunately, she struck up a friendship with a classmate (who still remains her best friend today), who encouraged Bholi to participate more confidently in class. Her day didn't stop after school though! Being the only sibling with a passion for cooking, Bholi would prepare the evening meals to ease some of the pressure from her mum. Since Bholi disliked cleaning, she delegated that task to her sister. Bholi watched her mum cook every type of subji (vegetable dish), pastry and dessert, and as a result, cooking came naturally to her.

Bholi enjoyed school (she was really fond of school dinners), but seeing that her family were struggling financially, she made a bold decision to leave education at the age of 15. She saw her mum, who had never had to work in India, exhausted after long shifts at a clothing factory, and decided that she would help the family by working alongside her mum. Bholi also enrolled on evening tailoring classes at the local college, to improve her skills and pursue her hobby. She's a very talented knitter, and makes the most creative blankets and garments for her family and friends – they are a real work of art.

At the age of 21, in 1973, Bholi found employment at a local factory, where she worked until the age of 52. By 30, Bholi had become a full-time working mother-of-three, but had also lost her dear father. With the help of her husband and a childminder, she juggled the daily duties that she held.

Bholi, or 'Gorgeous' to her granddaughter, is now a doting nanima to three (at the time of writing). She says her grandchildren mean the world to her. Today, she tries to live life to the fullest, going on trips

abroad, and spending more quality time with her family.

Quality time for Bholi also means gardening and tending to her treasured herbs, vegetables and beautiful flowers. Green-fingered Bholi is happiest when cooking with freshly picked herbs. She often takes the opportunity to teach her grandchildren about where food comes from and how it's grown. When I was cooking with Bholi, her husband was so helpful, doing background work behind the scenes. For example, he picked and washed the herbs, washed the heavy dishes when we were cooking, and lovingly fed her a cheeky bite of samosa whilst she was cooking. Despite all this, Bholi said he rarely praises her cooking to her face. Her husband is a man of actions, rather than romantic words. When I stayed for dinner one evening, I found it so sweet how they always ate dinner from the same plate.

Having spent a lot of time with Bholi, her organisational skills really shone through. Every single spice, pulse and pot has its own place in her recently-refurbished kitchen, clearly labelled of course. She owns an amazing collection of pots and pans, cooking gadgets, and every possible Indian spice. As I rummage her kitchen with wonder, she innocently smiles, calling her collection her one 'buying weakness'. I never once saw her looking stressed, as she multitasks in an effortless manner. Bholi emphasises how you should take time over cooking as it's one of life's pleasures. When she was making samosas, for example, she was originally going to use ready-made filo pastry to try and show me a shortcut. Within a few minutes of trying it, she refused to continue further as she didn't think it was good enough. She didn't blink an eye at making some fresh pastry dough, whereas I was encouraging her to save time. Bholi's daughters gave me a heads up before cooking with her, that she's all too good at hiding her top cooking secrets, and wished me luck in finding out! I saw it instantly, and Bholi kindly made me promise that I would only share her recipes once the book was published – 'these are my best secrets, I wouldn't just share them with anyone'. I kept her promise.

Bholi loves walking in the morning, and this gives her some quiet thinking time and personal space. She has a positive, can-do approach to life, where nothing is too much trouble. Incredibly kind and giving, Bholi invests a lot of time in supporting her children and grandchildren, and never hesitates to jump in the car to visit them and help where she can (even if it means getting lost along the way!)

The advice that Bholi would give to her grandchildren, when they are old enough to understand, is to keep your mother as your best friend. She stresses the importance of children being truthful and respectful to their mother, and that a mother will always give advice in her child's best interest.

Three of Bholi's recipes call for her favourite blend of cinnamon, green cardamom and brown cardamom. To save time when cooking her recipes, I grind this mix in advance and store in an airtight container. It's only required in small amounts in each recipe as a little goes a long way. As a guide, three quarters of a teaspoon of the powdered mix amounts to: seeds of two brown cardamoms, seeds of four green cardamoms, and one tiny stick of cinnamon (2cm). I'd recommend grinding the below in advance. If you prefer to grind as you go, I've specified the whole spices in the recipes.

- Seeds of 20 green cardamoms
- Seeds of 10 brown cardamoms (buy from Indian supermarkets)
- 1 large stick of cinnamon (around 2cm by 7cm)

Rajma
(Kidney beans)

Bholi's family love her rajma, and her daughters recommended it to me as another of their favourite dishes of hers. Her rajma is renowned for its creamy texture, rich taste and warmth. Bholi has adapted the traditional rajma recipe and made it creamier because she prefers a richer consistency. It's one which warms you up from the inside. She emphasises that some ingredients are optional, including the nuts, yoghurt and pomegranate powder, so feel free to alter according to your taste.

Bholi uses the slow cooker for this recipe. She switches it on to cook in the morning, and then goes for a walk and does some shopping! I prefer pressure cooking the rajma for convenience, and then simmering them so that they are just as delicious. Bholi approves of this method too. It goes without saying, but do take the relevant safety measures when using a pressure cooker. I allow the pressure to release naturally in the sink by pouring cold water on top and leaving it to stand before checking.

Perfect served with rice or a few chapattis.

Serves 5-6

300g raw kidney beans, washed and soaked overnight in approx 2 litres of water
1 and a half teaspoons salt (or to taste)
2 green finger chillies (or to taste)
1 large onion, chopped
200g tomato passata
4 almonds, soaked in water overnight and peeled (optional)
4 cashews, or 1 tablespoon pine nuts (optional)
2 tablespoons solid ghee (or around 4 tablespoons rapeseed oil)
4 cloves garlic
20g ginger, peeled and blended with the garlic
3 tablespoons plain natural yoghurt
Half teaspoon ground spice mix (see p63 for recipe) or grind together the spices below to a powder:
Seeds of 1 brown cardamom (optional)
Seeds of 2 green cardamoms
Tiny stick cinnamon (2cm)

1 level teaspoon red chilli powder (or to taste)
1 level teaspoon anardana (pomegranate powder)
Squirt of tomato purée or paste
Boiling water
Fresh coriander, to garnish

Prepare ahead: *The kidney beans and almonds require soaking overnight. I would also recommend preparing the ground spice mix in advance.*

Recipe continued overleaf.

Rajma (continued)

1. Wash the kidney beans and then soak in water overnight in your pressure cooker. Add half a teaspoon of salt and throw in the green chillies, pierced.
2. Pressure cook the kidney beans until soft and tender, but not mushy. To test, press one between your fingers and it should yield. It can take up to an hour to pressure cook these, depending on your pressure cooker.
3. If you haven't pre-made the spice mix, use a pestle and mortar to grind the seeds of the green cardamom, brown cardamom and cinnamon into a fine powder. Set aside.
4. Blend the cashews and almonds, with enough water to form a thick paste. Set aside.
5. Melt the ghee in a saucepan, then add the onions and cook until light brown, stirring regularly.
6. Add the garlic and ginger and cook for 2 minutes with the onions.
7. Add the tomatoes and cook over a medium heat, stirring regularly. Cook until the oil separates from the tomatoes as little bubbles.
8. Add the plain natural yoghurt, stirring as you do so.
9. Add the ground mix of cardamoms and cinnamon, the remaining teaspoon of salt, chilli powder, pomegranate powder, and the blended nuts. Keep stirring and add a squirt of tomato purée or paste.
10. Cook for 3-4 minutes over a medium heat, stirring regularly.
11. Add the cooked kidney beans to the tharka (masala base) and stir through. It should be a medium consistency with enough water to simmer.
12. If the consistency is on the thick side, add one to two cups of boiling water to the kidney beans, depending on your preferred consistency.
13. Stir and then simmer for 30 minutes, or until the sauce has thickened up to a medium consistency. Stir once or twice during this process to check on the consistency and ensure nothing is sticking to the base of the pan.
14. Cook over a medium-high heat, stirring frequently, until it reaches a medium consistency (or your preferred consistency).
15. Add coriander to garnish and serve hot.

"Bholi has adapted the traditional rajma recipe and made it creamier because she prefers a richer consistency. It's one which warms you up from the inside."

Aloo and mozzarella tikkis
(Potato fritters)

Bholi's carefully crafted version of the classic street food snack, aloo tikki, is a recipe I feel proud to share. As with all her recipes, it took a great deal of coaxing for Bholi to reveal her combination of ingredients. With all Bholi's herbs freshly picked from her garden, her kitchen was filled with wonderful aromas as we were preparing the mixture. What's so endearing about Bholi's cooking style is how she achieves a flavour which has undertones you can't quite put your finger on, because they all work together in a beautiful secret harmony. Her aloo tikkis are testament to that. The hints of mint and lime add a zest which uplifts the heaviness of the fried potato, whilst the pomegranate powder gives a subtle sweet and sour flavour. Best of all is the 'Mmm!' reaction you get from biting into a crispy tikki with a soft melted cheese centre. The way Bholi creates a filling is to slot the cheese in between two small tikkis (fritters) and unite them to form one large tikki. If you prefer no cheese or have an allergy or intolerance, you can fry the tikkis as they are without joining two together. Be aware – you'll make a lot more tikkis with this option, so adjust the size of your tikki according to preference.

A satisfying and filling tea snack or starter, aloo tikkis are delicious dunked in imlee chutney (see Indu's recipe on p176), mint chutney (see Sheila's recipe on p160) or just with a squirt of ketchup! For a more filling starter, serve with cholay (see Kamla's recipe on p196).

Makes 10 large aloo tikkis
To mix:
4 cloves garlic
20g ginger, peeled
Handful mint leaves
Handful coriander leaves
4 medium-sized white potatoes, boiled, peeled and mashed roughly
100g frozen peas, left to soak in water for 20 minutes then slightly mashed with hands (or sweetcorn)
Three quarter teaspoon red chilli powder, or to taste (alternatively,
blend fresh green chillies to taste)
Half teaspoon cumin seeds, dry roasted and then crushed to a powder with a pestle and mortar (optional)
1 heaped teaspoon garam masala
1 level teaspoon pomegranate powder
1 level teaspoon carom seeds (ajwain)
1 teaspoon Himalayan pink salt (or to taste) (You can buy this rose-pink salt from some supermarkets and
health food shops and it's Bholi's favourite. Alternatively, use normal salt)
Fresh juice of half a lime (or lemon)
2 tablespoons corn flour (this is different to cornmeal – corn flour is used here to help bind the mixture)

To cook:
200g grated mozzarella cheese (if buying ready grated bag, chop it really small)
Vegetable oil, for shallow frying

Recipe continued overleaf.

1. Blend the garlic and ginger finely and set aside. Next, roughly blend the mint and coriander and set aside.

2. In a large mixing bowl, add the potatoes and peas. Then add all remaining ingredients under 'to mix', except for the corn flour. Bholi prefers to use her hands for this as it helps gauge the texture, but you can use a spoon if you prefer.

3. Add the corn flour gradually, mixing in thoroughly so it's evenly spread. Corn flour helps to bind the mixture so that the tikkis don't come apart during cooking. As you add more corn flour, you should feel the mixture coming together as one piece. Use your judgement but try not to add too much.

4. Taste the mixture and add more spices to your liking.

5. Divide your mixture into 20 equal sized balls (two will join to make one tikki), weighing around 40-50g each. Exact weight will depend on the size of your potatoes.

6. Set out a bowl of water and dip your fingers into it. Hold your thumb and finger in a 'C' shape and rotate and flatten the ball using this shape to make a round tikki. Use your fingers to seal the edges so they are compact. The tikkis should be thick enough to take the filling (around 1cm depth).

7. Repeat for the rest of the balls.

8. Hold a tikki in one hand and make a pocket indent in the centre for the filling – keep the base thick though.

9. Place a small amount of mozzarella into this indent (I manage to squeeze in 1 teaspoon roughly – make sure the grated cheese is small). Place another tikki on top, making a single filled aloo tikki. Wet your fingers, then mould and flatten the tikki into a round shape as in step 6. Mine are usually 8cm diameter and about 1cm depth.

10. Repeat for the remaining tikkis.

11. Heat enough oil to coat the base of the pan and shallow fry – not too much as it will splatter. Place a plate lined with kitchen roll next to your frying pan ready to drain your freshly cooked aloo tikkis.

12. Once the oil is hot, carefully place a few tikkis in the pan and fry over a moderate-high heat. You should hear them sizzle if the oil is hot enough; if the oil gets too cool, the tikkis can absorb it, making them soggy. Leave a little gap between each one so that you have room to flip them.

13. Fry on one side for a few minutes until brown and crispy, then carefully turn the tikki using a spatula and fry on the other side.

14. Place the cooked tikkis on the kitchen roll and pat off any excess oil with another kitchen roll. Serve hot along with your chosen condiment, or cholay (chickpeas).

Freeze note: I prefer to freeze these in greaseproof paper, wrapped in clingfilm, to stop them from going soggy. Re-heat in the oven for best results.

Pea and potato samosas

Watching Bholi make her special samosas was a window into her years of culinary experience. She would calmly reach for her little bowls of freshly grown garlic and coriander, whilst mindfully cooking her filling and effortlessly shaping the samosas. All the while, her husband stood in the doorway looking on with admiration.

Bholi doesn't compromise when it comes to making samosas; she believes that the taste of the finished product makes the effort worthwhile, compared to shop-bought ones. She likes to make her own pastry, and prepare her filling using home-grown ingredients from her garden. Although she admits that making samosas is quite an art, and that shaping the samosas is quite fiddly, Bholi's advice to anyone new to making them is to stay calm and patient. It may take a few practice runs to perfect this one. To make life easier, Bholi suggests making samosas with a friend, and having a little production line going of the various steps involved. In Bholi's case, her nine-year-old granddaughter is always the first to volunteer!

Bholi has a secret tip for making the samosa cones easy to handle. Once the dough is rolled out into a circular round (shape), she lightly dry heats one side only, and this makes the cone sturdier when filling it. Another foolproof tip is to leave the cones to set for five minutes after sealing them with the flour paste. This gives the paste a chance to dry and seal, ready to take the filling.

Being vegetarian, Bholi loves the potato and pea filling given here, but for those meat-lovers amongst you, a keema filling (minced lamb) also goes down a treat (see Angela's recipe on p103). The samosa is a quintessential Indian snack, but it's also an ever-evolving one! The samosa's range of fillings and spice combinations have undergone years of transformation, from the Persian empires to the arrival of migrants in India.

Prepare ahead: You can prepare the dough the night before and leave it to set in the fridge, covered with clingfilm. I'd also recommend making the filling the night before and leaving it in the fridge.

Makes 10 samosas
Oil, for deep frying

For the pastry:
150g plain flour, plus extra for dusting
Half teaspoon salt (or to taste)
Half teaspoon carom seeds (ajwain) (optional)
Handful methi (fenugreek leaves), chopped (optional)
2 tablespoons rapeseed oil, plus half a teaspoon to coat dough storage bowl
70-80ml lukewarm water

Sealing paste:
1 tablespoon plain flour
Warm water (around 40ml, or enough to make a thick paste)

For the filling:
1 and a half tablespoons ghee (or 4 tablespoons rapeseed oil)
Half teaspoon cumin seeds
25g ginger, peeled and blended finely
3 cloves garlic, blended (optional)
Half a white onion, finely chopped
2 green finger chillies, finely chopped (or to taste)

100g frozen peas (or frozen peas/sweetcorn/carrot medley – make sure the pieces are small)
1 teaspoon garam masala
Half teaspoon pomegranate powder (or mango powder)
Half teaspoon paprika
Half teaspoon salt (or to taste)
Handful coriander, washed and finely chopped (including stalks)
1 medium-sized white potato (around 220-240g), boiled, peeled and grated (or equivalent weight with other variety of white potatoes)

1. Firstly, make the dough for the samosas. Add the plain flour, salt, carom seeds and fenugreek to a mixing bowl. Add the oil and rub into the flour with your fingers. Gradually add the water and mix to form a soft and moist dough.

2. Transfer the dough onto a clean surface, and knead for a few minutes until the consistency is smooth, elastic and firm.

Recipe continued overleaf.

3. Transfer the dough to a lightly oiled bowl and cover with clingfilm. Leave to set at room temperature whilst you cook the filling. If preparing the dough ahead of time, cover and refrigerate.

4. Now make the filling. Melt the ghee in a frying pan and add the cumin seeds, cooking them until they sizzle.

5. Stir in the ginger and garlic, and cook for a minute or two before adding onions and chillies. Cook until the onions are light brown.

6. Stir through the vegetables and cook until softened.

7. Stir in the spices and coriander and cook for 2 minutes.

8. Add the grated potatoes and stir, coating them fully in the masala. Set aside to cool.

9. Prepare your workstation for rolling out the dough. Dampen a tea towel and place it in the centre of a plate – this will keep the rolled-out dough moist. Lightly dust a clean work surface with plain flour. Now make the sealing paste for the samosa cones: mix the flour with warm water in a bowl to form a medium consistency paste. Set aside.

10. Divide the dough into 5 equal pieces (weighing approximately 40-50g each) and use the palms of your hands to roll each piece into a round ball.

11. Roll each ball into a thin round (shape) on your lightly floured surface. Aim for 1-1.5mm thickness and 13-14cm diameter (this is the art!). Roll, flip and rotate to help form a circle shape.

12. Heat one side of the round in a hot frying pan for around 20 seconds. Place the round in the damp tea towel. Stack so that you know which side has been heated, as this side will be the inside of the samosa.

13. Repeat steps 11 and 12 for the remaining dough balls. Then, slice the rounds in half to form two semicircles.

14. Take one semicircle. Tilt your palm horizontally and place a semicircle on it, circular side facing downwards.

15. Fold the top right corner into the bottom centre so that it forms a triangle, and hold there.

16. With your other hand, rub the sealing paste along that straight edge which you are holding. Also rub the paste along the straight edge which has not yet been folded down.

17. Fold the left-hand corner into the bottom centre, so that the pasted edges overlap to form a cone. Seal firmly with your fingertips by pressing down from the tip of the cone to the end of the seal so that there are no gaps. Rub and press paste onto the inside of the cone too. At this stage, your cone should be well formed with a tight seal.

18. Place the sealed, empty cone on a tray to set, whilst you make the other cones. Repeat stages 14-17 to make the remaining cones.

19. Sit one cone sturdily between your fingers, open side up. Put around 2 teaspoons of filling into the cone. Leave space to seal the top edge.

20. Rub the sealing paste inside the open edges. Firmly seal the pasted edges by pinching closed with your fingers. Fork down the sealed edge for extra sealing and presentation! Lay flat on a tray ready to fry.

21. Repeat steps 19-20 to fill the remainder of the cones.

22. Heat the oil for deep frying.

23. Test if the oil is hot enough by dropping in a tiny ball of dough. It should rise to the top fairly quickly. Line a plate with kitchen roll for the fried samosas – this will absorb excess oil.

24. Fry the samosas in batches until golden brown and crispy. Keep the heat moderate-high. Turn occasionally with a slotted spoon during this process. Drain off excess oil before placing on lined plate.

25. Enjoy hot, and serve with fresh mint chutney or imlee (tamarind) chutney (see recipes in this book).

Freeze note: Because this is quite a time-consuming recipe, it makes sense to cook a larger batch to freeze (scale up accordingly). If you don't plan on serving all the samosas, freeze them before frying, wrapped in greaseproof paper. I slightly thaw them before deep frying. You can also freeze fried samosas, and I like to oven-cook these straight from frozen.

Khoya

Khoya (also called mawa) is a dairy product made by boiling and simmering milk until it reduces to milk solids. This requires some tender loving care and lots of stirring over the cooker, but it's well worth a little effort. Unlike homemade paneer, which is also made from milk, you don't add a curdling ingredient to khoya. Because of this secret ingredient's creamy texture and taste, it's traditionally added to Indian sweets. As you'll see, Bholi likes to add khoya to her barfi and gajrela, and this is what gives them that extra creaminess, dadima-style!

I've found khoya tricky to get hold of – not all Indian supermarkets stock it. There are alternative khoya recipes out there which combine full fat milk powder and milk, but I prefer the original, old-school method if I'm going to do it from scratch. This is the recipe I've given below. You can make khoya whilst pottering around the kitchen or making another dish – you just need to keep an eye on it and stir regularly at the beginning, then quite vigorously towards the end when it reduces. The secret to making dadima-style khoya is to melt a little ghee (or butter) at the beginning to stop the milk from sticking. Use a heavy-based non-stick pan to reduce the likelihood of the milk burning or sticking, and keep the heat low to moderate.

Bholi's gajrela and barfi recipes each call for two handfuls of khoya, but I make extra as it is more economical to do so. The quantity below takes me 1 hour and 20 minutes from start to finish.

Prepare ahead: You can prepare khoya a few days in advance of cooking your gajrela or barfi, as it keeps well in the fridge; just freeze the amount that you won't need. If preparing on the same day as cooking the sweets, allow to cool, refrigerate for an hour and then grate ready for use.

Makes approximately 230g of
khoya
1 tablespoon ghee or unsalted butter
1 litre full fat milk

1. Melt the ghee in a saucepan.
2. Add the milk and bring to a gentle boil over a moderate heat. Stir regularly during this time.
3. Continue cooking over a moderate heat and stir regularly, making sure that you free up any milk solids gathering at the bottom of the pan.
4. After 35-40 minutes, you should find that the milk liquid has reduced significantly. Keep stirring over a moderate heat – the mixture should now feel like a lumpy liquid.
5. Lower the heat to a brave simmer now, as the milk can easily burn at this stage. Cook for 20 minutes or so, stirring regularly as more of the liquid is cooked off. It will look mushy and you should feel some resistance whilst stirring.
6. Cook until the liquid around the mixture has boiled off. Stir constantly at this stage and keep the heat fairly low. You'll know when it's done when the mixture comes together in one stir and slides around the pan easily.
7. Transfer to a flat plate and allow to cool for an hour to an hour and a half. Grate so that it's ready for use. If preparing desserts later in the day, store in the fridge and freeze what you don't need that day.

Freeze note: Khoya keeps well in the fridge for up to three days if you plan on making two desserts. Alternatively, freeze in bags and use within a few weeks.

Gorgeous gajrela
(Carrot halwa)

Bholi takes immense pride in preparing her version of this classic dessert, made with grated carrots. Gajrela, or gajar ka halwa, is a pudding known to mark celebrations, and Bholi brings that celebratory spirit to her everyday life. Knowing that her children and grandchildren light up when they taste her gajrela, Bholi doesn't think twice about preparing it for their visits, welcoming them with a hot slice of gajrela and a little dollop of vanilla ice cream. The great thing about this dish is that it keeps well for a few days in the fridge, and also freezes well – which is a useful cushion when you want to prepare ahead for a dinner party.

Bholi has tried to tweak her recipe to use less ghee. Her children, knowing how she loves to cook her Indian food in ghee, teased her that she should try to make it a little less of a guilty pleasure! Keen for the challenge, Bholi quietly went away and experimented according to their advice, only to find that her beloved gajrela now had a mildly burnt undertone. When I asked to try some, she told me that she was disappointed in herself for this batch, and that she was not going to take on board her children's advice again! (For the record, it still tasted delicious!) Bholi is a complete perfectionist, and never fails to surprise me with her nuggets of culinary know-how, which she just shrugs off with a smile.

As with her barfi, Bholi uses the dried milk product, khoya, in her gajrela. It's the secret to giving it a slightly creamy taste, as well as an even consistency. It's time-consuming to make at home, but totally worth the effort. You can buy it from some Indian stores as a fresh block, but you'll find the homemade recipe here just in case (see khoya recipe on p74).

I would recommend using a large, heavy-based karahi or a round-based, heavy non-stick pan.

Serves 7-8 when cut into small chunks

Three quarter teaspoon ground spice mix plus a pinch more for garnish (see p63), or grind together the spices below to a powder:
1 tiny stick of cinnamon
Seeds of 2 brown cardamoms
Seeds of 4 green cardamoms

2 and a half tablespoons solid ghee (or unsalted butter)
1kg peeled, grated carrots

500ml full fat milk
120g white sugar (or to taste)
2 handfuls grated khoya
2 tablespoons roughly ground pistachios, plus a few chopped for garnish – around 10 ground and 2 chopped)
12 almonds (soak 8 overnight in water, then peel and crush, and keep 4 aside to chop for garnish)
1 and a half tablespoons melon seeds (available in packets from Indian supermarkets)

You will need: *A spice grinder (or pestle and mortar), greaseproof paper, ideally a spatula to move the mixture around the pan and stop anything from sticking to the pan.*

Prepare ahead: *It's useful to prepare the ground spice mix ahead of time. The almonds require soaking overnight.*

Recipe continued overleaf.

1. If you haven't pre-made the spice mix, grind the cinnamon and cardamoms to a powder using a pestle and mortar (remove the shells). Keep a good pinch aside for garnish; the rest we'll add whilst cooking.
2. Melt the ghee in your karahi, or frying pan, over a moderate heat.
3. Add the grated carrots over a medium heat, moving them around the pan as you are adding. You should see the water from the carrots being released into the pan.
4. Use the spatula to keep moving the carrots around the pan. Do this until the excess water has cooked off.
5. Gradually add the milk, stirring as you do so.
6. Cook for around 30 minutes, stirring regularly, until the carrots have absorbed the milk. They should look glazed and little bubbles of ghee will appear around the gajrela.
7. Add the ground spice mix and stir together for a few minutes.
8. Add the sugar and khoya and stir until the texture has softened.
9. Add the pistachios, almonds and melon seeds. Stir through until they have softened.
10. Once the mixture has come together, without excess liquid, transfer into a dish lined with greaseproof paper. Level out with a spatula and garnish with the remaining chopped nuts and a pinch of ground spice mix.
11. Allow to cool for at least 1 hour before slicing up into chunks. Serve hot with ice cream.

Freeze note: Freeze any leftovers (if any!) in greaseproof paper, wrapped in clingfilm. Thaw and re-heat in the microwave.

"Bholi uses the dried milk product khoya in her gajrela. It's the secret to giving it a slightly creamy taste, as well as an even consistency. It's time-consuming to make at home, but totally worth the effort."

Mango kulfi
(Ice cream)

Kulfi, a delicious dairy dessert associated with South Asia, is often likened to ice cream. It's not quite the same as an ice cream due to its dense texture, taste and method of preparation. Like ice cream, though, kulfi comes in many different flavours, and Bholi's favourite is mango with a hint of pistachios. Traditionally, kulfi is made by boiling, simmering and reducing the volume of milk, which is a time-consuming process. So I was intrigued when Bholi showed me her modern no-cook kulfi recipe, which is so easy to make and doesn't compromise on taste.

Bholi uses the pulp of fresh, sweet mangoes. She buys hers from her local South Asian supermarket as she likes to pick the thin-skinned, juicy varieties from India and Pakistan. I've used tinned mango pulp here for ease and convenience. However, if you do wish to use fresh mangoes, make sure they are very ripe before making into a pulp and add sugar to taste. I've substituted fresh milk, for condensed milk and evaporated milk. After experimenting with different combinations, I found the latter option gave the best results for texture and taste. Whilst Bholi adds her beloved ground spice mix of brown cardamom, green cardamom and cinnamon, I have just used green cardamoms.

Bholi recommends having all of the ingredients and containers set out so that the mango mixture can be smoothly returned to the freezer as soon as it's done. Her top piece of advice is to ensure that the mixture is whisked thoroughly in advance of pouring it into the freezing containers. If you do not attend to this, ice crystals may form in the kulfi.

I've found it tricky to get hold of the cone-shaped moulds traditionally used for kulfi. You can buy them from certain Indian supermarkets, or order them online. However, following Bholi's example, I prefer using small and practical storage tubs or jelly moulds. If they're good enough for the kitchen gadget queen, they're good enough for me! They're economical, widely available and easy to slot into the ice cube compartment of your freezer – just make sure they are freezer safe and have lids (otherwise the exposed surface crystallizes). As odd as it sounds, I've found that the 150ml food storage containers meant for baby food storage, as well as the 150ml jelly moulds, are perfect for kulfi. I've given measurements here to make a batch of kulfi, purely because it's so easy to do in one go, meaning it's one less thing to worry about when guests come over.

Prepare ahead: This is the perfect dessert if you're planning ahead for a dinner party. You can prepare it a good month in advance, and the only thing you'll need to do on the day is remove from the mould.

See the mango kulfi recipe overleaf.

Mango kulfi (continued)

Makes approximately 1.5 litres of kulfi (10 servings in 150ml moulds)
400ml whipping cream
397g condensed milk (1 tin)
410g evaporated milk (1 tin)
400g tinned mango pulp, ideally of the Alphonso or Gir Kesar varieties
Seeds of 3 green cardamom pods

(shells discarded), ground to a powder
Handful of pistachios, chopped

You will need: *Kulfi moulds or freezer-safe pots with lids, an electric hand whisk (or a manual one if you're feeling strong!)*

1. Prepare your workstation. Set out your clean and dry containers/moulds, and take out a jug.
2. Add the whipping cream to a large mixing bowl and whisk until smooth.
3. Whisk in the condensed milk and evaporated milk.
4. Add the mango pulp and cardamom powder. Whisk for a few minutes until really smooth.
5. Transfer to a jug and then pour into your containers, ready for freezing.
6. Garnish each kulfi with chopped pistachios and pop the lid on.
7. Allow to set in the freezer overnight (or a minimum of 6 hours).
8. To remove a kulfi portion from a small plastic container: place the tub in a bowl of hot water, which sits below the lid, for 1-2 minutes. Squeeze the sides of the tub to loosen the mould and tip upside down onto your serving dish (follow instructions on your chosen mould if using alternative storage). Because kulfi has a dense texture, allow to stand for a minute before serving so it softens.
9. Enjoy as a dessert by itself or with a warm slice of Bholi's gajrela (carrot halwa) for extra indulgence.

Almond and pistachio barfi

Make barfi on a day you're feeling indulgent and in need of a little sweetness. It also helps if you're in a generous mood as this classic sweet dish is a sociable one. Known as mithai in Punjabi, barfi is traditionally enjoyed in small quantities to mark special occasions, but it's also a superstar sweet to welcome guests along with samosas, pakoras and a mug of masala chai. There are many types of barfi, and the one I share below is Bholi's prized recipe – in the case of this one, I haven't made any tweaks to it at all.

Bholi always has a batch of barfi at the ready when her children and little grandchildren come to visit her. Her daughter, pregnant at the time of writing, is particularly grateful for the sweet treat! Bholi lovingly packs parcels of barfi for them to take away.

As you'll notice from some of Bholi's other recipes, she likes to use crushed and soaked nuts in her cooking as a natural method of adding creaminess. If you prefer not to use nuts, you can add desiccated coconut instead, or dried fruits, raisins or currants.

One of the secrets to making barfi like Bholi is to keep watch over your mixture so that it doesn't burn. Keep the heat moderate to control the temperature. Bholi has a weakness for buying pots and pans, and always opts for her non-stick karahi for barfi. If you don't have one, use a wide, heavy-based non-stick pan. Barfi requires your full attention, and this recipe needs a lot of stirring. If you want to have a bit of fun, mould your barfi into heart shapes, like I've done in the pictures shown here, as a gift! Just be sure to do this when the barfi is still warm. Alternatively, cut it into little chunks to spread the love.

Makes about 20 little squares
3 tablespoons solid ghee
500g dry milk powder
Three quarters of a tin evaporated milk (around 300g)
5 tablespoons crushed pistachios, plus 1 tablespoon whole pistachios for garnish
18 almonds (soak 14 overnight in water. Then peel and crush, and keep 4 aside to chop for garnish)
2 tablespoons melon seeds (you can buy these in packets from Indian supermarkets)
Three quarter teaspoon ground spice mix (see p63). Or grind together the ingredients below to a smooth powder:
2 brown cardamoms, shells removed
4 green cardamoms, shells removed
1 tiny stick cinnamon
200g white sugar, ground in a spice grinder, or 200g caster sugar
2 big handfuls grated khoya

Prepare ahead: *It's useful to prepare the ground spice mix ahead of time. The almonds require soaking overnight.*

Recipe continued overleaf.

Almond and pistachio barfi (continued)

1. Before starting, line a shallow tray with greaseproof paper (my square tray is around 4cm depth and 24cm width) and set aside.

2. Tip the milk powder into a mixing bowl, and gradually add three quarters of the tin of evaporated milk, mixing by hand; it will be a bit clumpy. Then add however much you need of the remaining quarter of the tin to make the mixture moist and soft to the touch. Bholi recommends adding the evaporated milk gradually so that you have greater control.

3. Melt the ghee in a pan.

4. Add the crushed pistachios and almonds. Stir for a few minutes over a low-moderate heat, so that all of the nuts are coated. The aroma should be being released now, and you'll see little bubbles around the mixture.

5. At this point, add the melon seeds to the pan and stir until they have softened slightly.

6. Add half a teaspoon of the ground spice mix – it's best to add less of this first as ground spices have an intense flavour. Stir constantly over a medium heat.

7. Add the milk mixture into the pan, mixing as you do.

8. Keep stirring and mashing the contents of the pan to get rid of the lumps. As it cooks further, you will see a more even consistency where the mixture comes together. Keep going until you see little bubbles appearing around the mixture where the ghee is being released.

9. Slowly add the sugar – too fast and it can form lumps! As you add more sugar, be sure to remove any lumps first.

10. Taste the mixture for sweetness and spices. Add more of the spice mix to taste (I always do).

11. Once your mixture is as smooth as you can make it, add the grated khoya (if using). Mix until the texture softens and the barfi slides around the pan easily as one lump. At this stage, switch off the heat – we don't want it to burn.

12. Pour the barfi mix into your lined tray. Smooth the top and push into the edges, as you would with a cake.

13. Whilst it's warm, slice up the almonds and pistachios kept aside for garnish, and sprinkle on top.

14. At this stage, I sometimes use a mould if I want to make my barfi look a bit fancy – a heart shape, for example, as shown here. Leave the barfi to cool for at least 2 hours before removing the mould. Bholi doesn't do this, however, so if you want to follow her lead, simply leave the barfi to cool for 2 hours before cutting into small, dainty squares. Then share and enjoy!

Angela

mung daal
simple salmon fillets
fusion salmon
aubergine bharta
keema
methi chicken
crispy chicken thighs

ngela is a warm, loving and doting dadima, but life hasn't always been plain sailing for her. With hindsight, she believes her hardships have shaped her into the strong woman that she is today. Her advice to a younger generation is "Don't be afraid of making mistakes, as the challenges you face in your life will help you grow into a stronger, more confident person".

When I first explained the idea behind my book to Angela, she was full of enthusiasm about sharing her experiences with me. I was really touched when she sent me a handwritten letter, giving me some background about her life. Her letter painted a very moving picture, and when I later met her in person, she brought that story to life for me.

During the early 1950s, young Angela and her family were caught up in a period of political upheaval in India. Angela, her parents, and three siblings, fled the surrounding violence and journeyed to the UK by boat. Her parents were young at the time, and unfamiliar with the English language. They were hard-working and decided to build a new life in Leeds, since they already had family based there. Angela's upbringing in Leeds was a humble one. As her family grew, she became one of seven siblings. Angela remembers some of the hardships vividly, and how her house was cold and damp. She soon discovered that hand-me-down clothes, no holidays, no eating out, and no non-food related shopping trips, were the norms for her family at that particular time.

Food evokes special memories for Angela: the economic use of ingredients, and the anticipation of tucking into her mum's cooking with a rumbling stomach. It was these memories that made Angela see the struggle that her parents went through, to feed a family of nine. Her parents always put a meal on the table, however modest it may have been. Angela recalls running through the front door after school and being hit with the familiar aroma of her mum's freshly cooked jeera rice (rice with cumin seeds). Angela would dash into the kitchen with her coat still on, eagerly lift the lid of the large pan, and scoop a spoon of steaming rice into a bowl when no-one was looking. Sometimes Angela would be pleasantly surprised to come home to the sweet scent of milky semiyan (a sweet dish made from vermicelli pasta – see Santosh's recipe on p57) or kheer (rice pudding). When her mum wasn't around, Angela's mother-hen sister would cater to Angela's British tastebuds. She would prepare her favourite after-school snack: bread and butter smeared with strawberry jam.

Angela's dad was the breadwinner, who worked his socks off as a salesman, whilst her mum took charge of the home. Although Angela's mum was always rushed off her feet, she had her little helpers. Young Angela and her sisters would shoulder the domestic duties, whilst their brothers enjoyed a more leisurely lifestyle! Angela was happy to help her mum, especially if it involved sampling her Indian cooking. She remembers how her relatives would spontaneously pop in for tea – something very common in the Indian culture. Angela watched and learnt from her mum, who resourcefully rustled up meals for guests, and welcomed them into her home with warmth. To Angela's delight, it was always sizzling hot pakoras (bhajis) on the menu – they were easy to share, and perfect as a tea-time treat. Angela would pick a few and make a pakora sandwich, adding a generous squirt of tomato ketchup. Another benefit of helping her mum in the kitchen, was knowing where to find the stash of macaroon biscuits, kept exclusively for guests! "The kettle was never off!" Angela says. I can see where Angela gets her hospitable nature from. During my visits, including Angela's photoshoot, cups of tea were always at the ready, and food plentiful.

Apart from seeing her mother cook with care, young Angela was also moved by the skilled cooking of other women. In particular, on her first visit to the Gurdwara (Sikh place of worship). Angela saw the hours of preparation which went into 'langar' (a daily meal for all visitors to the temple, free of charge and prepared by volunteers). She remembers walking down a stone staircase, into the hustle and bustle of women cooking and talking, whilst stirring a huge steaming pan of daal and tossing rotis (chapattis). Angela's mum explained how the volunteers offered their cooking talents, to prepare langar. Angela was

Cooking keema

inspired by the love and care that the volunteers invested in making this special meal for the general public. She loved visiting the Gurdwara and enjoyed the delicious food. Angela felt so inspired that she always volunteered to serve food to the congregation.

Alongside her love for traditional Indian food, Angela loved English school dinners, as they had a real novelty factor. When the lunchtime bell rang, her growling stomach would feel comforted by the thought of those large aluminium trays, which offered root vegetables, meat pies, roast potatoes, and other hearty fare. Angela found the British classics just as comforting as her mum's Indian food. Angela's daughter-in-law tells me that she always looks forward to her mother-in-law's Christmas dinner, and that Angela is in her element whilst preparing a feast for everyone, with a small sherry to hand. Angela's daughter-in-law adds that her mother-in-law has a small obsession with potatoes! Apparently, one Christmas, the fridge was full of potatoes, as Angela was worried about not having enough.

It's not at all surprising that Angela likes to be organised and prepared, as she was used to shouldering responsibility from a young age. As a teenager, Angela saw financial circumstances toughen in her family. As a result, her mum was determined to master the English language, learn how to drive a van, and set up an outdoor market stall. Angela and her sisters would take it in turns to help their mum – even if this meant taking the odd cheeky Friday off school! It was worth it for their treat of fish and chips with scallops on their way home.

It was all well and good that Angela was so helpful. However, in a hectic household, where making ends meet was a top priority, nobody ever asked Angela what she wanted to do with her life. At school, Angela felt that she lacked encouragement from her teachers. She loved science, and shared her dream to become a teacher with her teacher, but was greeted with the advice that she was better suited to being a secretary or typist! Angela recalls having to share a tarnished textbook, and determinedly thinking: 'If I could just get my hands on that book myself, I'll show them what I can do!' And she did! When she become a science teacher later in life, she made a point of visiting her old school and telling the teacher who had doubted her.

However, without guidance, time to study, or any worldly experience, Angela's journey required perseverance and resilience. With little time to study, Angela didn't get the grades needed to go on to further education. Nonetheless, she re-sat her O-levels, and then took up evening classes to complete her A-levels (all whilst juggling household jobs and the family business). Having secured the grades, Angela then had to master how to apply for teaching. It was only after overhearing other students discussing their applications, that she learnt what to do. She was successful and began studying for her Certificate of Education. A year into her course, Angela learnt that helping at home, plus commuting and making time to study, was out of the question. Exhausted after catching two buses every day with a heavy pile of books, Angela realised how hard she had it compared to students who lived on campus. For her final two years, Angela invested in her education and lived on campus during the weekdays.

The next challenge was getting a job in teaching. Forty or so applications later, Angela secured a job as a chemistry teacher in Manchester. She still remembers the new striped dress she wore for her interview, how she woke up at 4am to get two trains and a bus, and how she was shaking with excitement when she secured the job. Unfortunately, except for her dad, the family never shared her excitement. Although she was 24, Angela had lived a sheltered life up till then. It was a huge deal moving away from home, and she quickly learnt how to stand up for herself when people were ignorant of her culture.

One day, her father called her at work, to tell her that she was being introduced to a potential suitor. Angela was against the idea, and told her dad that she would wear the scruffiest clothes possible to put him off! But when she met her future husband, the twinkle in his eye won her over. Her husband was raised in India and loved Indian food. Angela's husband praises her cooking, and is always happy to

Marinating the methi chicken

prep ingredients for her, or add a cheeky spoon of ghee to her daal when she's not looking!

Angela has become increasingly health-conscious (although not obsessive), particularly after she had a lump removed from her pancreas. With Angela's grandson, son, and daughter-in-law living just around the corner from her, she batch cooks Indian food as a way of helping them with their busy lives. Angela was never a fussy eater and would eat anything that was given to her – including the dessert 'sago', affectionately called frogs' spawn at school (a dessert which other schoolchildren hated!). Sharing memories of her dad bringing home chickens with their feathers on, she laughs at the fact that her son can't stand eating meat on the bone.

Apart from cooking for her own children, Angela thinks very carefully about the food she cooks for her young grandson, whether it's a piece of grilled fish with steamed vegetables and baby potatoes, or roast chicken. She and her husband work as a team to have their grandson's dinner ready as soon as he's back after school – Angela gives her husband a call, and he heats up the food so there is no time for the little one to get distracted with toys! Angela feels that part of the reason for the current child obesity epidemic, is that children are not being filled up on the 'right' type of foods – they are not eating enough fibrous food. After a trip to the cinema with her grandson, Angela rustled up a 'pronti' (a Punjabi word for a little paratha, or flatbread) with scrambled eggs and yoghurt, and even threw in some ajwain (carom seeds) so he would get used to their taste. She was proud of the fact that he 'wolfed it down' and didn't ask for anything else for the rest of the afternoon!

Although Angela now spends a lot of time at home, she used to juggle work and cooking, amongst other responsibilities. She believes that you can always find time to cook, even within a busy full-time job and family – it's all about planning ahead and preparation, she stresses.

Angela believes that it is crucial to pass on recipes, not just from an older generation to a younger one, but across age groups. Here, I pass on Angela's culinary knowledge, with a few personal twists here and there. Hopefully, you'll do the same, and pass them along to your nearest and dearest.

Mung daal
(Yellow lentils)

Angela showed me how she cooks her version of mung daal on a Tuesday. Although Angela is renowned in the family for her tasty meat dishes, on Tuesdays (a special day of a Hindu goddess) she and her family eat vegetarian food for religious reasons.

Whilst I was cooking this dish with Angela, she talked nostalgically about her humble childhood in Leeds, and how eating this daal connects her with those special memories. When she was a young girl, Angela's mum would call her in for dinner after playing outside, and on the table would sit a big pot of yellow mung daal, with a stack of warm rotis, smeared in butter. Her mum cooked simple food, using inexpensive ingredients, with the few pots and pans she had brought to England from India.

Angela's sister-in-law, a skilled cook who lives in India, taught her how to perfect mung daal during her early years of marriage. Her sister-in-law advised her to use fewer spices to bring out the key flavours.

I loved Angela's daal, but I've added more flavours in line with my own preference. I've included tomatoes, garlic, ginger, garam masala and green chillies to give it more of a spicy kick. Angela also mixes ghee and olive oil at the start, but I've just used ghee. Angela likes to add a pinch of asafoetida (hing) as it's supposedly great for digestion – only add a pinch if you do use it, as it has a pungent taste, not to everyone's liking (my mum, for example, hates the smell).

I've added another personal preference of mine, based on my mum's and dadima's cooking style, and that's to combine mung with masoor daal (split red lentils). The method is the same as Angela's, but the masoor daal adds another colour, flavour and texture. Instead of a mustard yellow, as in the photograph, mung masoor daal would look more orange.

There are so many varieties of lentils, which are often used in different forms and combinations in North Indian cooking and this can make the buying process a little confusing. Yellow mung daal refers to the green mung beans which have been split and had the skins removed. Masoor daal is split red lentils. You can buy these from some mainstream supermarkets in the world foods section, and in good Indian supermarkets.

See the mung daal recipe overleaf.

Mung daal (continued)

Serves 4-6

*400g mung daal, washed thoroughly
(or 200g mung daal and 200g
masoor daal mixed together)
Approximately 1.5 litres of water
(add more if you like a runnier daal)
1 and a half teaspoons haldi
(turmeric powder)*

*2 teaspoons salt (or to taste)
1 and a half tablespoons solid ghee
1 teaspoon cumin seeds
1 large onion, chopped
2 green finger chillies, finely chopped
(or to taste)
4 cloves garlic, chopped
20g ginger, peeled and grated*

*1 teaspoon coriander powder
Pinch of hing (asafoetida) (optional)
1 teaspoon garam masala
150g blended plum tomatoes
Handful fresh coriander, washed
and finely chopped (reserve some for
garnish)
Knob of butter (optional)*

1. Pour the lentils into a deep stock pan filled with 1.5 litres of water and turn on the heat. Add the haldi and 1 teaspoon of the salt as soon as the water is lukewarm, then stir.

2. Bring to the boil. As the daal is boiling, remove the frothy white layer which forms at the top of the water – just scoop it off into a bowl.

3. When the water has come to a boil, lower the heat and simmer for around 15 minutes, stirring occasionally.

4. In the meantime, make a start on the tharka (masala base). Melt the ghee in a separate pan over a moderate heat.

5. Add the cumin seeds and allow to sizzle for a few seconds before adding the chopped onions and green chillies.

6. Cook until the onions are light brown, stirring regularly, then add the garlic and ginger.

7. Add the coriander powder, pinch of hing (if using) and garam masala.

8. Stir well over a medium heat for 2 minutes and then add the tomatoes.

9. Cook and stir until the tharka has come together, or until little bubbles form around the mixture.

10. Add the freshly chopped coriander to the tharka.

11. Give the daal a stir to check if the lentils are fully cooked; they should have absorbed most of the water and gone soft. If they haven't, keep simmering until the daal becomes a medium-thick consistency. I like my daal quite thick, but feel free to add more boiling water if you prefer a runnier texture.

12. Pour the pan of tharka into the daal and mix well; you will see the colour change. To pick up all of the tharka flavours, Angela's trick is to pour a large spoon of daal back into the tharka pan and swirl it around. Pour this back into the daal and stir well.

13. Simmer for a further couple of minutes, or until the daal has reached a medium consistency again.

14. Taste the daal for spices, and add the remaining teaspoon of salt, to personal preference.

15. Garnish with fresh coriander and add a knob of butter for that beautiful creamy taste. Serve piping hot with rotis.

Freeze note: This daal freezes well in an airtight container once cooled. For best taste, I always re-heat it in a saucepan, and add a little boiling water to loosen up the lentils and revive their texture. When re-heating it, I also like to recreate that fresh taste by adding some lightly fried onions.

Simple salmon fillets

These salmon fillets are so simple to prepare, which makes them the perfect weeknight meal or starter. It's just a case of coating them in marinade, wrapping them in foil, and then sliding them into a hot oven. Angela recommends using skin-on salmon, as it helps the fillet to stay compact during cooking, and seals in the marinade.

I've changed Angela's original recipe and used my own marinade, but stuck with oven-baking the salmon as Angela does. For a light and refreshing starter, I tend to halve the fillets (if they're large) and serve them on a bed of baby leaf salad and red onions, garnished with pomegranate. If serving as a main dish, couple with vegetable rice and a subji (vegetable dish) of your choice.

This dish is super simple – just remember to marinate your fillets for at least 30 minutes before cooking (I usually leave them overnight), and not to overcook them.

Serves 4 as a main course or 6-8
as a starter
4 fillets boneless skin-on salmon

Marinade:
6-7 tablespoons rapeseed oil

Juice of 1 squeezed lime or lemon
1 teaspoon paprika
Half teaspoon red chilli powder (or
to taste)
1 heaped teaspoon ground black
pepper

1. Wash the salmon and pat dry with a kitchen roll. Leave aside.
2. Mix your marinade ingredients in a small bowl and then transfer onto a plate.
3. Place the first fillet of salmon on your marinating plate, coating all sides; ease it into the grooves of the salmon with your fingers. Repeat for the remaining fillets – add more oil and spices to your marinade if it's running low.
4. Place all the fillets on the marinating plate and cover over with clingfilm. Leave in the fridge to marinate for a minimum of 30 minutes, or overnight if you're preparing ahead.
5. Pre-heat your oven to 180°C and prepare 4 pieces of foil, big enough to wrap up each fillet individually.
6. Wrap each fillet individually in the foil parcel and fold over at the top – leave plenty of space around the salmon.
7. Oven cook on the middle shelf of the oven for 15 minutes. Serve hot.

Fusion salmon

Angela's original dish is a fusion of exciting flavours, and I've honoured that when tweaking her recipe. She likes the saltiness of soy sauce, the zing of lemon, and the kick of Indian spices. Her salmon dish is one of her son's favourites after the gym.

When I learnt this dish from Angela, and had the pleasure of joining her extended family for dinner, she served it on a bed of jeera rice with her yellow mung daal, keema, bharta and rotis (see recipes in this book).

I've swapped cooking oil for virgin coconut oil, as it makes a wonderful base when the flavours melt and merge. To help bind the spices and mellow any pungency from the salmon, I've also added a dash of runny honey to the marinade. Whilst Angela likes the salty and zingy combo of light soy sauce, dark soy sauce and fish sauce, I have chosen dark soy sauce for simplicity.

If you're going to serve this with other dishes, I recommend subtle accompaniments which won't overpower the salmon – yellow mung daal is therefore a good option, as is a vibrant green veg like bhindi (okra) or aloo palak (potatoes and fenugreek). Yoghurt is not generally served with salmon – it's just not the done thing in my experience.

Serves 4
4 skinless and boneless salmon fillets (not smoked)
Rapeseed oil, to cook
Fresh coriander, to garnish

For the marinade:
Quarter teaspoon chilli powder
Half teaspoon turmeric powder
1 and a half teaspoons runny honey

For the tharka:
1 and a half tablespoons solid virgin coconut oil (or 4 tablespoons rapeseed oil)
1 teaspoon mustard seeds
20g ginger, peeled and grated
4 cloves garlic, chopped
1 green finger chilli, finely chopped (or to taste)
2 small onions (or one large), chopped

Half teaspoon salt (or to taste)
Half teaspoon coriander powder
Juice of half a lime (or lemon if you prefer)
1 teaspoon dark soy sauce
Boiling water
Coriander, to garnish

1. Wash the salmon and pat dry with a kitchen roll – we don't want excess water in our marinade. Chop into ice-cube sized chunks (so they are small enough for the flavour to infuse, but not too small that they break when added to the sauce). Set aside in a mixing bowl.

2. Add the chilli powder, turmeric powder and honey. Gently mix, being careful not to break the salmon. Cover over and refrigerate for a minimum of 30 minutes (or a few hours earlier if you're preparing ahead).

3. In the meantime, cook the tharka. Melt the coconut oil over a low heat, then add the mustard seeds. Wait for them to start sizzling and making a popping sound, then add the ginger, garlic and green chillies. Stir for a minute.

4. Stir in the onions and cook over a moderate heat until light brown. Add the salt and coriander powder. Add a splash of water to the tharka to stop it from sticking if required.

5. Add the lime juice and dark soy sauce and mix well.

6. Pour half a cup of boiling water onto your onion tharka – add more if you prefer a runnier consistency. Stir for a few minutes over a moderate heat until little bubbles form around the mixture.

7. At this stage, Angela likes to 'seal' the salmon chunks so that they are ready for the sauce. In a separate frying pan, heat 2 tablespoons of rapeseed oil and add the marinated salmon. Gently toss the salmon once or twice over a medium-high heat for just 1 minute.

8. Once the salmon looks like it's building up a thin coating around it, but is still not fully changing colour, transfer to your tharka pan. Stir carefully or simply shuffle your pan using the handle. At this point, add a little more boiling water – just enough to loosen the consistency.

9. Cover with a lid and simmer for 10 minutes.

10. Uncover, turn up the heat and allow most of the excess liquid to boil off whilst carefully stirring regularly. You should see small bubbles around the salmon where the liquid is boiling off.

11. Once it's a medium consistency, take off the heat, garnish with the coriander and serve immediately.

"I've swapped cooking oil for virgin coconut oil, as it makes a wonderful base when the flavours melt and merge. I've also added a dash of runny honey to the marinade."

Aubergine bharta
(Mashed aubergines with peas)

Bharta is the Punjabi word which refers to a dish of cooked, mashed vegetables in a tharka. I found myself cooking bharta a lot when I lived in Madrid – on my daily trips to the greengrocers, I was always drawn to the plump and glossy aubergines. They would remind me of when my mum would roast a batch of them, and the kitchen would be filled with their smoky aroma. Whilst I was living abroad, I regularly texted my family photos of the food I was cooking. They would tease me about how often they received photos of my bharta! It's one of those dishes which is so easy to prepare ahead, cook and freeze.

Sometimes aubergines can have a bitter undertone to them. Angela's simple reminder is to drain excess liquid from the roasted aubergines – she finds this helps to take out that bitter edge. Angela's other tip is to not overdo it with the tomatoes – after all, the aubergine is the hero of this dish. For the quantity below, I recommend just under half a tin of chopped tomatoes (around 180g). I've specified chopped tomatoes and onions, as I find this adds texture to the fleshy, mashed aubergines. Angela doesn't add peas, but I have added them below for a burst of colour and also, their delicate sweetness. I've also added a dash of tomato purée to lift the colour of the tharka away from being too brown.

Prepare ahead: I would recommend roasting, peeling and mashing the aubergines in advance of making bharta. Do this up to a day ahead, or a few hours before cooking. Refrigerate in an airtight container until needed.

Serves 4-5 as a side dish
2 regular-sized aubergines
4 tablespoons rapeseed oil
1 teaspoon cumin seeds
1 onion, diced into chunks
4 cloves garlic, finely chopped

1 heaped tablespoon grated ginger
2 green finger chillies, finely chopped
(or to taste)
Half teaspoon salt (or to taste)
Three quarter teaspoon coriander
powder

Three quarter teaspoon paprika
180g tinned chopped tomatoes
Squirt of tomato purée
120g frozen peas
1 teaspoon garam masala
Freshly chopped coriander, to garnish

1. First of all, prepare the aubergines. Roast them in a hot oven, on the middle rack, at 180°C. Cook for 20-30 minutes, or until the skins are glazed, shrivelled and soft. Turn once during cooking. When the aubergines can be pierced easily with a knife, remove from the oven and leave to cool. When cool enough to handle, slice off the crown of the aubergine and peel off the skin. Fork through the pulp so that it's mashed. Drain excess liquid through a colander, and set aside whilst you prepare the tharka.
2. Heat the oil and add the cumin seeds, cooking until they sizzle.
3. Add the onions and stir for 4-5 minutes over a moderate heat, until light brown.
4. Stir in the garlic, ginger and green chillies and cook for 2 minutes. Then stir in the salt, coriander powder and paprika, making sure the onions are coated.
5. Cook for 1-2 minutes and then add the tomatoes. Stir regularly over a moderate-high heat until the tharka is done. This is when the oil bubbles separate from the tomatoes around the edge of the mixture. Then stir in the tomato purée. Add the peas and cook for 5 minutes, or until softened.
6. Add the mashed aubergines. Stir, making sure the aubergines are coated in the tharka. Cook for a further 5 minutes. Taste and add more salt if needed. Stir in the garam masala, garnish with the coriander and serve hot.

Freeze note: If you have aubergines to use up, but don't want to make bharta on the day, freeze the pulp in an airtight container. Follow step 1 of the recipe, leave the mashed pulp to cool, then freeze. This is a great time-saver. To cook, thaw out the frozen aubergine pulp, and add to the tharka as per recipe.

Keema
(Minced lamb)

Angela's keema is a hit with her family, so she always makes a large quantity in anticipation of them wanting second helpings! Knowing that her children have busy working lives, Angela helps out by sending keema for them to freeze. I can relate to Angela's gesture, as my mum and dad would lovingly prepare keema for my sister and I when we lived out during our university years. They would be very competitive over who cooks it the best!

Angela believes that the flavours in keema should be robust enough for the meat. She creates a full-bodied tharka by 'bhunning' (browning) the onions well, and by adding whole spices for a while. Angela's preference is to remove the whole spices once they've released their flavour – she doesn't like the idea of her guests having to pick them out! Angela's keema has a luscious, succulent texture. This is achieved through cooking off the excess juices of the meat, and then simmering gently.

Whilst Angela likes to add a dollop of natural yoghurt to her keema, I've not included this in the recipe below, as I like the rich taste of the meat as it is. I've also tweaked the recipe to use fresh green chillies, as opposed to powdered chilli. The addition of peas is down to preference, although Angela likes to use them. Depending on who I'm cooking for, I add or omit them (as you'll see from the photo, I used them that day). I have not included them in the recipe below, but feel free to add.

If you have leftovers, keema makes a great filling for stuffed peppers (see Kamla's stuffed peppers on p202), and parathas (see Sheila's aloo parathas recipe on p143) or samosas (see Bholi's recipe on p71). Keema really is quite versatile – if you fancied mixing up cuisines a bit, you could serve it with spaghetti and sprinkle over some Parmesan as a kind of Indian spaghetti Bolognese! My sister loves this!

Angela prefers to use a stainless steel karahi for this dish. If you don't have one, a wide heavy-based pan will work just as well.

Serves 4
1 and a half tablespoons solid ghee, or 4 tablespoons rapeseed oil
1 teaspoon cumin seeds
4 cloves garlic, blended finely
25g peeled ginger, blended finely with the garlic
1 large onion, diced
Three quarter teaspoon salt (or to taste)
1 teaspoon turmeric powder (haldi)
1 level teaspoon coriander powder (optional)

Half teaspoon paprika
2 green finger chillies, finely chopped (or to taste)
500g lean minced lamb meat
200g blended plum tomatoes
Squirt of tomato purée
Approx 300ml boiling water
1 teaspoon garam masala
Quarter teaspoon cumin seeds, dry roasted and then ground to a powder, to garnish (optional)
Handful freshly chopped coriander, to garnish

Whole spices (to be removed during cooking):
2 bay leaves
2 brown cardamoms
3 green cardamoms
1 small stick cinnamon
3 cloves
1 dried red chilli

Recipe continued overleaf.

1. Melt the ghee and add the cumin seeds, cooking until they sizzle.
2. Stir in the garlic and ginger, coating in ghee. Keep the heat low so that it doesn't spit too much.
3. Add the whole spices and cover for 2 minutes.
4. Add the onions, coating them in ghee. Cover, lower the heat, and cook until medium brown – this can take a good 10-12 minutes. You will need to stir occasionally, and add splashes of water, to ensure that nothing sticks to the pan.
5. Once the onions have browned, add the salt, turmeric powder, coriander powder, paprika and green chillies. Add a splash of water to protect the spices from burning.
6. Stir well, coating the onions in the spices. Cook for 2-3 minutes, stirring regularly.
7. Stir in the mince over a medium heat. Use your spoon to break up the individual mince pieces. Stir again to ensure all pieces are fully coated with onions and spices.
8. Stir the mince frequently for 15 minutes, or until the excess liquid disappears, and it's almost cooked. It's best not to leave the cooker unattended for this stage.
9. Add the tomatoes and tomato purée and stir through, coating the mince. Cook until the meat has absorbed the tomatoes; look out for the oil bubbles forming around the mixture where the oil has separated from the tomatoes. This is the secret to knowing when the tharka has cooked with the meat. During this time, use tongs to pick out any whole spices you can find. It's not the end of the world if you don't find all of them – you can pick more out as and when you see them.
10. Now that the tharka and meat are ready, it's time to simmer. Add around 300ml of boiling water, or just enough that it sits just below the top of the meat. Stir well.
11. Cover and simmer for a good 15-20 minutes, then stir.
12. Simmer for a further 10 minutes until the mince has softened and most of the water has been absorbed.
13. Over a high heat now, stir the keema to cook off excess water. Once ready, it should look as if the tharka and meat have bound together. Stir through the garam masala and ground cumin seeds.
14. Garnish with the coriander and serve piping hot.

Freeze note: Keema freezes well. Re-heating in the microwave just doesn't do it justice though – it gives it a dry, rubbery texture. For best results, thaw and re-heat in a saucepan over a low heat. Add a little boiling water to loosen up the mince and revive the colour.

"My mum and dad would lovingly prepare keema for my sister and I when we lived at university. They would be very competitive over who cooks it the best!"

Methi chicken

This dish is Angela's go-to when she has guests over for dinner, or when she's cooking for her family who have very particular tastes. Even though a lot of methi is not used in this dish, Angela calls this dish methi (fenugreek) chicken because she loves the aromatic flavour it adds to the meat. Angela loves being inspired by cookery programmes, and whilst cooking, she often whips out her notepad to jot down new ideas – something her husband finds really sweet and funny! These little tips from cookery shows, combined with her regular visits to India, have inspired this tried and tested recipe for marinated chicken thighs.

Here are the secret tips for making this dish, which I managed to coax out of Angela. Use chicken thigh meat as it's a succulent cut. Secondly, it is worth the effort to dry roast the cumin seeds and then roughly grind them in a pestle and mortar – it adds a delightful kick. Take time to really bhun (brown) the onions before adding the meat. Finally, add natural yoghurt, but not too much as it can be overpowering.

Although Angela uses butter mixed with oil to cook this dish, I prefer ghee. Angela is a big fan of cooking meat on the bone for added flavour, as this is what she grew up with. I always make this dish using boneless chicken thighs, however, for convenience. The succulence of the thigh meat can hold its own. To save time, ask your butcher to chop the thighs into lean chunks for you.

With this dish, the marinating does most of the hard work for you. I find the cooking part enjoyable and easy, allowing me to multi-task around the kitchen.

Cook in a wide-based lidded pan or a karahi. Perfect served with steaming hot vegetable rice and yoghurt.

Serves 6-7
To marinate:
10 boneless and skinless chicken thighs, chopped into chunks
1 teaspoon turmeric powder
1 teaspoon coriander powder
1 teaspoon garam masala
Half teaspoon red chilli powder (or to taste)
Half teaspoon salt, to taste
3 green finger chillies, finely chopped

(or to taste)
6 cloves garlic, finely chopped
40g ginger, peeled and grated
Half teaspoon cumin seeds, dry roasted until fragrant then ground to a powder
3 level tablespoons natural yoghurt

To cook:
2 tablespoons solid ghee or unsalted butter

2 onions, diced
2 handfuls fresh fenugreek leaves, finely chopped or blended (or 2 tablespoons dried fenugreek leaves sold as kasuri methi in Indian supermarkets – soak in water for 10 minutes before adding)
1-2 cups boiling water
1 green pepper, chopped into chunks
Handful coriander, to garnish

Recipe continued overleaf.

Methi chicken (continued)

1. Add all the ingredients listed under 'To marinate' to a mixing bowl. Mix using your hands, making sure the chicken is completely coated (be sure to wash your hands afterwards as the mixture contains spices).
2. Cover with clingfilm and marinate overnight in the fridge, if you have time, or for a minimum of 1 hour.
3. Melt the ghee in a pan over a low heat, then add the onions. Cover and cook until medium-dark brown, stirring occasionally. Add a splash of water if necessary to ensure nothing sticks.
4. Stir in the marinated chicken and cook over a high heat for 2 minutes, mixing well with the onions.
5. Add the methi. If using dried methi, drain it through a fine sieve or tea strainer and add to the chicken. Stir.
6. Now we need to cook off the juices. Stir the chicken regularly over a medium-high heat, until the excess liquid has bubbled away.
7. Time to simmer the chicken. Add a cup of boiling water to loosen the consistency – add another half cup if necessary. Cover and simmer over a low heat for 15 minutes. Stir halfway through to check nothing is sticking.
8. Add the chopped peppers, cover and simmer for a further 10-15 minutes, or until the water has reduced by about half and the chicken is cooked.
9. Stir uncovered over a high heat for a further 10 minutes or until the water has cooked off. Turn off the heat – we don't want to dry out the meat. Consistency-wise, the tharka should be a coating which clings to the chicken rather than a sauce.
10. Garnish with fresh coriander and serve immediately.

"The marinating does most of the hard work for you, so the cooking part is really just enjoyable, not messy and allows for easy multi-tasking around the kitchen."

Crispy chicken thighs

Angela is all for simple, good quality meat and fish dishes. These baked chicken thighs are effortless to make – the marinating and oven do all the work for you. Angela's original recipe is mild, as it caters for her four-year-old grandson and pregnant daughter-in-law. It's a real hit with both of them. I've spiced up the marinade and added garlic, more chilli powder and a dash of soy sauce for colour and glaze, something my mum does.

If you're cooking for the kids and they don't like spice, omit the chilli powder altogether and reduce the spices accordingly. Tastes great served on a bed of salad for a light meal, or with daal and rice. Like Angela's simple salmon fillets, the key is to marinate first. Angela likes to seal the meat over a high heat on a griddle pan, and then oven cook.

Serves 4-6
You will need: *a griddle pan (or non-stick frying pan)*

6 plump chicken thighs, skin-on, bone in (or boneless if you prefer)

Marinade:
7 tablespoons rapeseed oil
Juice of 1 lemon
1 tablespoon dark soy sauce
5 medium-sized cloves garlic, crushed

1 teaspoon paprika
1 teaspoon salt (or to taste)
Half teaspoon ground black pepper
Half teaspoon red chilli powder

1. Mix the marinade ingredients in a mixing bowl (large enough to add the thighs and wide enough for them to sit at the base).
2. Add the chicken thighs and smother in the marinade, ensuring the meat is fully coated. Place skin side down in the marinade and refrigerate overnight, or minimum 1 hour.
3. When you are ready to cook, heat a griddle pan (or non-stick frying pan).
4. Sear the chicken, skin side down, until you see the skin darken and crisp slightly. Turn over and heat the other side. Only turn once – we're just sealing in the marinade, not cooking it through.
5. Place on a baking tray in a hot oven at 180°C, on the middle rack, and bake for 40 minutes to 1 hour. Check the meat after 30 minutes. The juices and oils should have released and the skin should be nice and crispy. Remove from the oven when the meat is pierced easily with a knife and has cooked through. Use a spoon to coat the chicken with the juices from the baking tray and serve immediately.

Arun

green mung and chana daal
bhindi – no strings attached
arun's rice
courgette and baby corn subji
corn on the cob subji
vegetable koftas
dahi bhalle

However busy life gets, you can't beat home-cooked food. Try to batch cook, freeze and plan ahead.

run started cooking at a young age for her family. I spent a lot of time watching her cook, and during the process, I saw how those early culinary experiences have given her real confidence in how she approaches cooking in such a calm manner. As she was teaching me dishes, she was also simmering masala chai, and preparing ingredients with great skill and poise. As the eldest of six, she played a strong maternal role in the family's upbringing, and would regularly cook dinner for her five younger siblings while her parents were busy running their off-licence business.

Raised in West London during the late 1960s, Arun and her siblings were a lively bunch of children, who enjoyed playing outdoors. Unlike her younger siblings, however, Arun couldn't afford to be as carefree as she had many responsibilities. Today, Arun's siblings have genuine admiration and respect for their older sister, and appreciate the sacrifices that she made for them during her girlhood.

When her parents worked during the school summer holidays, Arun would coordinate the meals for her siblings, and then divide the workload for the day with her younger sister. They would clean the house, plate the food, and clear up after dinner. Cheese on toast with curried beans (a British-Indian fusion dish which many Indians grew up on as an alternative subji) regularly featured on the menu, along with anything else that they could creatively cook with the ingredients at home.

Arun talked about the importance of experimenting with different flavours in the same dish, and not being afraid to take risks with food. She places great emphasis on good homemade cooking, rather than fast food and eating out at restaurants.

With her marriage at 18, Arun learnt how to cook more sophisticated Indian dishes than curried beans! Impressively, her learning was all very independent. Vegetarian dishes were on the menu every day, in line with their religious beliefs. Used to experimenting with ingredients, Arun got creative with flavour combinations for different lentils, vegetables, Indian breads and accompaniments. Arun looks back with a smile at her cookery blips from those early days of marriage. Cooking fresh food daily, she learnt swiftly through trial and error and relied on her gut instinct, knowledge and feedback from her family to perfect her dishes.

Given Arun's experimental learning, it makes sense that she believes that when preparing good food for the family, you should never over-analyse the recipe or process. When cooking and exploring new flavours, also be guided by your instinct, passion and personal tastes (as well as the tastes of your guests). Arun's culinary creations might include a handful of pomegranate seeds, a chunk of creamed coconut, or even a squirt of tomato ketchup in chilli paneer! She has many cooking secrets, to name but a few: a little mango powder adds a zingy twist to dishes, a squirt of lemon juice brings out the colour of okra, and squeezing out water from vegetables is the secret to great koftas. She has a relaxed yet impressively skilled approach, gained through years of experience, and a willingness to experiment. "It's difficult to tell someone how to cook something," she says. "Even with daal, I don't think 'where's my measuring jug?' or 'I need 500g of this or 200g of that'. You just use your judgement, pour it out and mix it together!" (I can vouch for this – I watched and studied Arun's cooking techniques, but left all measuring to my own kitchen!)

Although laid-back in her attitude towards cooking, Arun is highly organised when it comes to planning ahead. As a young nanima to three granddaughters, and working full-time, Arun makes home-cooking suit her lifestyle today. She doesn't believe in slaving over the cooker when you can make life easier by batch-cooking and freezing – meals are convenient, accessible and far healthier this way! After rummaging through her freezer, I saw forward planning in full glory. There were ice trays filled with freshly-blitzed garlic, ginger and green chillies, herbs chopped and frozen etcetera. If guests turned up on her doorstep, she would not feel stressed about cooking them a great Indian meal.

Arun loves a good bargain, and buys fresh ingredients in advance, when cheaper and in season. This helps with freezing and planning ahead. Arun is also passionate about growing vegetables in her garden, and she definitely has green fingers! She takes time to teach her granddaughters about the importance of growing vegetables, so that they can continue with healthy eating habits later in life. As a young girl and married woman, money was tight at times, so Arun learnt to cook good food resourcefully, within a budget.

Although very laid back in her cooking style, Arun is quite the back-seat chef when it comes to watching her family cook – all in good jest, Arun cannot resist sharing what she would do differently!

Arun's kitchen wisdom is now travelling even further down the generational line, as she teaches her granddaughters the art of cooking. When they visit for sleepovers, she makes fresh pizza with them, giving each their own child-size rolling pin and dough. The most important ingredient, however, is the freedom to squeeze, roll and flour to their heart's content. Mess does not enter the equation – for Arun, it's all about those precious childhood moments of learning, experimenting and having fun! Arun loves how her granddaughters enjoy eating Indian food, especially their menu requests and compliments: "Nani (nan), we want your daal roti today!"

Arun is a natural cook, who makes it look so easy. Her girlhood experiences have shaped her passionate and relaxed approach to preparing food for the family. Her culinary advice to young cooks? "Take time to watch and learn, and don't be afraid to experiment with flavours and ingredients. You can't beat home-cooked food and it's not that hard if you plan ahead!" With that encouragement from Arun, I leave you to some creative cooking with her dishes.

Green mung and chana

Green mung and chana daal
(Green daal and split chickpea daal)

This daal is a family favourite in Arun's home, and one which she has been making for years. Arun loves to prepare a large batch before visiting her daughter, as she knows that her three little granddaughters will happily enjoy it with rice. Arun's technique is to pressure cook the lentils, and make the tharka (onion masala base) separately. It goes without saying, but do take the relevant safety precautions when using a pressure cooker.

Arun's advice is to take your time with the tharka, as this is the 'make-or-break' element of the dish, and to always simmer the daal once the tharka has been added to it.

Serves 6
For pressure cooking the lentils:
250g green mung daal
200g chana daal
1-1.3 litres of water
4 garlic cloves, left whole
1 teaspoon salt (or to taste)

For the tharka:
4 tablespoons rapeseed oil

1 heaped teaspoon cumin seeds
1 large onion, chopped
25g fresh ginger, peeled and grated
2 green finger chillies, finely chopped
(or to taste)
1 heaped teaspoon turmeric powder
Half teaspoon salt (or to taste)
Half teaspoon black pepper
Half teaspoon paprika
1 level teaspoon coriander powder

1 teaspoon garam masala
250g tomato passata
Fresh coriander, to garnish

Freeze note: *Freeze in an airtight container. Re-heat in a saucepan with a little boiling water to loosen the consistency.*

1. Check the lentils and remove any stones or grit, if any. Wash thoroughly.
2. Put the lentils into a pressure cooker along with 1.1 litres of water, garlic and salt.
3. Pressure cook over a moderate heat until the lentils are soft to the touch. Exact times will depend on your appliance – I pressure cook the daal for approximately 20-30 minutes, for a good few whistles.
4. Check the lentils are cooked: allow the pressure to release (I pour cold water over the pressure cooker in the sink, and leave to stand) before opening the lid. Stir and check whether the lentils have softened – particularly the chana daal as this takes longer to cook than mung. It should be a medium consistency with enough excess water for simmering. If it's on the thick side, add boiling water accordingly (around 150ml-200ml should be fine). Never add cold water at this stage.
5. Simmer the daal uncovered and without the pressure (as if it were a standard saucepan) whilst you cook the tharka. Depending on the size of your pressure cooker, you may wish to transfer to a separate pan for the simmering.
6. Heat the oil in a saucepan, then add cumin seeds and wait for them to sizzle before adding the onions.
7. Cook the onions over a medium heat until soft and light brown. Stir regularly.
8. Stir in the ginger and green chillies and cook for 2 minutes with the onions. Then add all of the spices.
9. Cook the spices for 2 minutes with the onions, stirring regularly. Then stir through the tomato passata.
10. Cook the tharka until it is ready. This is when oil bubbles appear around the tharka and the sauce consistency thickens.
11. Pour the tharka into the cooked lentils and stir through. Add 1 cup of boiling water to the daal (or more if you prefer a thinner daal) so that it can be simmered.
12. Simmer for 20 minutes until it reaches a medium consistency. Stir occasionally. Garnish with fresh coriander and serve hot.

Bhindi –
No strings attached

Okra, also known as 'ladies fingers' or bhindi in Punjabi, is another one of those vegetables (like karele – bitter gourd) with an acquired taste. If you've cooked with okra before, you'll know that these nutrient-rich pods can have a gooey and slimy texture. This is the mucilage or fluid produced by the okra plant, found in many other plants including aloe vera. With the right cooking conditions, that off-putting texture disappears – so don't be dissuaded from enjoying this much-loved Indian delicacy!

For Arun, it's no secret that okra is a great source of vitamins, folates and fibre – her mum shared this knowledge with her as a young girl. But that's not the reason why she loves okra. Arun has perfected a straightforward and foolproof method, which makes cooking okra a pleasure.

When buying okra, Arun is really particular (just like my dadima!) and prefers to choose her own loose vegetables, rather than buying them pre-packed. Here are Arun's tips for buying okra:

- Choose okra which is firm when pinched, not limp and soft – the tip should snap off crisply. Be careful a shop assistant isn't watching though...!
- Go for the brighter green ones (rather than ones with lots of brown spots) as they tend to be fresher.
- Size-wise, the smaller pods are younger and cook quicker, which is best for this dish.

Now for Arun's cooking secrets:
- Arun's number one rule is that the okra should have no water or excess moisture. After washing them, dry carefully with a kitchen roll – the drier the better.
- Don't use any tomatoes.
- Do not cut the okra into small slices, as this exposes more of the slimy texture. Instead, Arun always 'tops and tails' her okra and then slices each piece through the middle into two long strips, or sometimes just three-quarters of the way through so that the pod flaps open slightly.
- Once you've cut your okra strips, and if you have time, leave them out for 15 minutes or so to dry even more.
- Cook the okra by itself, over a fairly high heat, and cook the tharka (onion masala) separately. Once they are each cooked, combine them briefly and serve immediately. This is Arun's tried and tested technique for no strings.
- Always cook okra in an uncovered frying pan – ideally a wide-based one.
- During cooking, add a dash of freshly squeezed lemon or lime juice. Apart from reducing the slimy texture, Arun says that the citrus juice helps to retain the okra's vibrant green colour.
- Slice the onions into chunky slices – this is Arun's preference for presentation.
- Do not add salt until the very end. Salt draws out liquid, and we want to avoid any excess moisture.

See the bhindi recipe overleaf.

Bhindi (continued)

Serves 3-4 as a side dish
5 tablespoons rapeseed oil (2 tablespoons to cook the okra, 3 tablespoons for the tharka)
200g okra, washed and patted dry with a kitchen roll, topped and tailed, then sliced through the middle

1 white onion, sliced to medium thickness
3 cloves garlic, finely chopped
2 green finger chillies, finely chopped (or to taste)
1 teaspoon haldi (turmeric powder)
1 quarter teaspoon amchoor (mango powder), or anardana

(pomegranate powder)
1 teaspoon garam masala
1 teaspoon freshly squeezed lemon or lime juice
Half teaspoon salt (or to taste)
Fresh coriander, to garnish
Handful of pomegranate seeds, to garnish (optional)

1. Heat around 2 tablespoons of the oil in a heavy-based frying pan. Ensure your okra is fully dry then add to the hot oil.
2. Cook the okra over a fairly high heat until soft and tender, but still firm. You should be able to pierce it with a knife. Stir regularly.
3. Transfer the okra to a plate and set aside whilst you make the tharka (onion masala base).
4. In the same saucepan, heat the remaining 3 tablespoons of oil (you may need less depending on your pan and how much grease you have left). Cook the onions over a medium heat until light brown. Then stir through the garlic and green chillies for 1 minute.
5. Add the haldi, mango powder and garam masala, coating the onions fully. Cook and stir over a low heat for 2 minutes.
6. Stir in the okra over a fairly high heat until it's coated fully with the tharka. Then add the lemon juice over the okra and stir for 1 minute (only needs a quick heat as the okra was cooked earlier).
7. Turn of the heat, add salt to taste and stir through whilst hot. Garnish with fresh coriander and pomegranate. Serve immediately. Best enjoyed fresh.

"Choose okra which is firm when pinched, not limp and soft – the tip should snap off crisply. Be careful a shop assistant isn't watching

Arun's rice

Rice is seen as a 'simple' staple dish, but there's a real art to making it fluffy, with separate grains which effortlessly fall from a spoon. Like rotis, mastering perfect rice-making takes experience, and everyone has their own techniques. Some people like soaking the rice beforehand, using their finger to measure the depth of water, and using foil to steam cook the grains and let them sit. The experienced dadimas in this book make cooking rice look easy. It's been tricky pinning down their measurements of water and the exact ratio of water to rice – they tend to gauge the correct amount of water by sight, and never time the rice, but seem to know instinctively when it's done. I've used cups and grams as measurements here.

Arun uses basmati white rice and is thorough when it comes to washing out the starch. Her secret is to wash her rice before and after cooking, and she boils it in a pan of loose water (roughly four mugs of water to one mug of rice) so there's no need for precise measuring. There are two parts to this dish: cooking the rice, and then in a separate pan, preparing the seasoning to which the rice is added. The trick is to avoid over-stirring, and when you do, use a flat spatula to stir around the edges and flick into the middle of the pan. It's important to use a wide saucepan – the rice needs plenty of room so that it doesn't become clogged and mushy.

At family gatherings, Arun's family always wait for her to arrive so that she can make the rice her way – they all know how fussy she is, and how she will end up being a 'back-seat cook' if she is forced to watch someone else cook it! I've shared three simple variations of Arun's rice below. The method for each is very similar, so I've just included the different seasonings as separate methods.

Plain rice:

1 cup basmati rice (around 300g)
Water, to boil the rice
Salt, to taste
Knob of butter

Jeera (cumin seeds) seasoning:

1 and a half tablespoons solid ghee (or 4 tablespoons rapeseed oil)
2 teaspoons cumin seeds
2 brown cardamoms, crushed open (optional)
1 small stick cinnamon (optional)
Salt, to taste

Mixed vegetables:

4 tablespoons rapeseed oil
1 teaspoon cumin seeds
150g frozen mixed vegetables (or any fresh vegetable of your choice-chopped small)
Salt, to taste
The following spices are optional:
2 bay leaves
Half teaspoon ground black pepper
Half teaspoon paprika
Quarter teaspoon red chilli powder
Half teaspoon garam masala

Recipe continued overleaf.

Plain rice:

1. Wash the rice in a saucepan – use the same saucepan that you will use to boil the rice. Fill the pan up with water, swirl it around with your hands and carefully tip out the cloudy water. Repeat until the water runs clear. If you prefer to use a fine sieve, be sure to place a mixing bowl underneath so that you can tell when the water runs clear.

2. Soak the rice in a saucepan of cold loose water for 30 minutes – no longer than this.

3. Bring to the boil, uncovered.

4. When the water is bubbling, reduce the heat to the lowest simmer, and give it one good stir. Then simmer for 10 minutes, or until the rice is almost cooked.

5. Remove one grain of rice and test if it breaks easily using a spoon. It should almost be there.

6. Simmer for a further 5 minutes until the rice is soft to the touch.

7. Check the rice again for softness – it should now be done. Don't worry if there is still water in the saucepan – we're boiling in loose water, not exact quantities.

8. Drain the rice through a sieve and wash under running warm/hot water.

9. Sit the sieve on your saucepan and set aside whilst you prepare the seasoning for the rice (see below).

10. For plain rice, simply transfer it into a serving dish, add salt to taste, and carefully stir through a knob of butter (use a spoon or fork so it doesn't crush the grains).

Jeera rice seasoning:

1. Melt the ghee in a wide, non-stick frying pan which is big enough for the rice to be tipped into afterwards.

2. Add the cumin seeds to the ghee. Once they are sizzling and have slightly darkened in colour, stir through the brown cardamom and cinnamon. Once fragrant, it's ready for the rice.

3. Shake off any excess water from the rice and tip it into the seasoning. Add salt to taste. Stir over a high heat just once or twice so the rice is heated through and glazed with the seasoning.

4. Turn off the heat, remove the whole spices if you wish, and serve immediately.

Mixed vegetables (spices optional):

1. Heat the oil in a wide, non-stick frying pan which is big enough for the rice to be tipped into afterwards.

2. Add the cumin seeds to the hot oil. Once the cumin seeds are sizzling, add the mixed vegetables. Stir over a medium heat, coating them with oil.

3. After 5 minutes of cooking, add salt to taste, spices and bay leaves (if using). Stir through, coating the rice fully.

4. Cook until the vegetables are soft to the touch but firm, stirring regularly.

5. Shake off any excess water from the rice and tip it into the pan. Fold the seasoning and the vegetables through so that all the grains are coated.

6. Turn off the heat and serve immediately.

Courgette and baby corn subji

This subji (vegetable dish) is the perfect side dish to rustle up on a weeknight – it's flavoursome and easy to make. Arun makes this dish when she's in a relaxed, carefree mood. She doesn't like to fuss over the precise details of how her vegetables are cut – for Arun, chunks are chunks, and she hardly ever uses a chopping board! What Arun is fussy about, however, is flavour and texture. Arun advises that this should be a fairly dry subji with a coating of tharka (onion masala). She adds just enough tomatoes and water to cook the vegetables and give them a nice glaze. Arun adds baby corn for a splash of colour and to balance the soft courgettes with a delicate crunch. You could also use sweetcorn pieces or another vegetable of your choice.

Serves 4
4 tablespoons rapeseed oil
1 teaspoon cumin seeds
1 white onion, diced
3 cloves garlic, finely chopped
1 teaspoon turmeric powder (haldi)
1 level teaspoon coriander powder
Three quarter teaspoon salt (or to taste)
Half teaspoon paprika
1 green finger chilli, finely chopped (or to taste)

100g plum tomatoes, blended (about a quarter of a tin)
2 medium courgettes, washed and cut into medium-sized cubes
Half cup of boiling water
150g baby corn, chopped into halves
1 teaspoon garam masala
Coriander to garnish

You will need: *A heavy-based non-stick saucepan*

1. Heat the oil and then add cumin seeds, allowing them to sizzle.
2. Add the onions. Coat with the oil and cook over a medium heat until light brown and softened.
3. Add garlic and cook for 2 minutes, stirring regularly.
4. Add the haldi, coriander powder, salt, paprika and green chillies, coating the onions. Stir occasionally, over a low heat, for 2 minutes.
5. Add the tomatoes and cook over a medium heat until the tharka is ready. This is when the consistency thickens and oil bubbles form around the mixture.
6. Stir in the courgettes, then add half a cup of boiling water – or enough to coat the vegetables and loosen up the tharka.
7. Cover and simmer until the courgettes have started to soften. Stir occasionally in between to check there is no sticking.
8. Stir in the baby corn, cover and simmer for 20 minutes, or until all the vegetables have softened. Add the garam masala and stir through.
9. Garnish with coriander and serve with rotis, or on a bed of rice.

Corn on the cob subji

Arun's corn on the cob subji has to be one of my favourite recipes in this book. As you can see from the photo in this chapter, I didn't waste any time tucking in during our photoshoot break. This subji is perfect for those days when you feel like eating with no airs or graces, whilst having a laugh with your friends and family. Every bite is so juicy, luscious and fragrant, that it's well worth a bit of messy eating with your hands. Just don't wear a white top!

I've grown up calling this dish 'chalia', which is the Punjabi word for corn on the cob. Arun chops the corn into dainty little roundels, boils them, and then coats them in a creamy tharka. Arun also likes to add small pieces of loose sweetcorn for added texture to the tharka.

Serves 5-6
5 cloves garlic
30g fresh ginger, peeled
2 green finger chillies (or to taste)
4 frozen mini corn on the cobs,
thawed (around 550g)
100g frozen sweetcorn

2 teaspoons turmeric powder
4 and a half tablespoons rapeseed oil
1 white onion, finely blended
1 teaspoon salt (or to taste)
1 teaspoon ground black pepper
Three quarter teaspoon paprika,
plus quarter teaspoon for garnish

120g tomato passata
50g creamed coconut
Approximately half a cup boiling
water
Quarter teaspoon garam masala
Fresh coriander, to garnish

1. Blend the garlic, ginger and green chillies finely and set aside.
2. Use a large knife to chop the corn on the cob into roughly half-inch thick pieces (about 3-4 layers of corn per slice). If you've chopped this vegetable before, you'll know it's a tough one. Ensure it's thawed properly and use a large, heavy knife to apply pressure and make life easier for yourself.
3. Place the chopped corn on the cob and sweetcorn into a large cooking pot with loose cold water. Heat the water, once tepid add 1 teaspoon of the turmeric powder and stir. Bring to the boil.
4. In the meantime, make a start on the tharka. Heat the oil in a wide frying pan (big enough to take the corn on the cob) before adding the onions. Cook over a moderate heat until softened, stirring regularly.
5. Add the garlic, ginger and chillies. Cook with the onions until they are light brown, stirring occasionally. Once your corn on the cob has come to a boil, simmer on a low heat whilst you finish making the tharka.
6. Add the remaining turmeric powder, salt, pepper and paprika to the onions. Stir through, then cook for 2-3 minutes, stirring regularly.
7. Add the tomato passata and stir through. Cook over a moderate heat for 2-3 minutes.
8. Add the creamed coconut and stir through until it melts. Cook over a medium heat until the tharka has thickened.
9. Add half a cup of boiling water and stir over a medium heat until it becomes a medium consistency paste.
10. Add the corn on the cob pieces and the handful of frozen corn and stir through, coating each and every one with tharka.
11. Simmer over a low heat for 5-10 minutes until the tharka becomes a fairly thick coating – this is meant to be a juicy but fairly dry dish. Stir through garam masala.
12. Garnish with coriander and a pinch of paprika. Serve hot.

Vegetable koftas

Arun sums up her version of koftas well: "Eating these takes 2 minutes – it's the preparation which needs time and effort!" She is very particular when it comes to preparing her ingredients – her nightmare scenario would be bland koftas which break apart when fried. With this scenario in mind, she's developed tried and tested techniques which make flavoursome koftas. Arun always batch cooks her koftas and freezes ahead (without the sauce).

Arun's favourite filling to use is cauliflower – being vegetarian, she loves to use this versatile vegetable. In line with her younger daughter's tastes, Arun also uses combinations of spinach and paneer, mixed vegetables, cabbage or ghiya (bottle gourd). I love experimenting with these combinations.

Arun's secret to making koftas which bind well is to use a muslin cloth to really squeeze out the excess water. Arun never uses chilli powder in koftas, only fresh chillies. The key to the tharka (onion masala base) is to make it a smooth, medium consistency. Arun uses a hand-blender to achieve this.

When it comes to serving the koftas, always stir them into the sauce just before serving – too early and they will go soggy. Try and serve the koftas in a fairly shallow dish, so that they are slightly propped up in the thick, creamy sauce and you can see the top of them.

Serves 4-5
For the koftas:
30g ginger, peeled
3 green finger chillies, topped (or to taste)
Half teaspoon cumin seeds
Handful fresh fenugreek, washed and left to dry
Handful fresh coriander, washed and left to dry
1 medium-sized cauliflower, washed and grated (remove leaves, chop in half and grate as normal)
1 teaspoon garam masala
1 teaspoon ground black pepper
1 teaspoon salt (or to taste)
Vegetable oil for deep frying
2 big handfuls gram flour (chickpea flour/besan), plus 1 extra handful to add gradually
1 teaspoon corn flour

1. Blend the ginger and green chillies finely. Set aside.
2. Dry roast the cumin seeds until fragrant. Crush to a powder using a pestle and mortar and set aside.
3. Roughly blend the fenugreek and coriander so they look finely chopped. Set aside.
4. Remove excess water from the grated cauliflower (or any other vegetable you use): place the grated cauliflower into the centre of a muslin cloth (do this in two batches if you think there is too much at once); fold in the edges, making a little 'sack' so that nothing falls out; then, holding the gap closed with one hand, use your other hand to squeeze out excess water over the sink. Don't be tempted to skip this step.
5. Transfer the squeezed cauliflower into a large mixing bowl. The texture should have changed and become like a solid lump.
6. Add the ginger, green chillies, coriander, fenugreek and all spices except for salt. Mix well with your hands or a wooden spoon. Add the salt now – it's best to add it last, as it draws out water.
7. Heat oil for deep frying.

Recipe continued overleaf.

Vegetable koftas (continued)

8. In the meantime, add two handfuls of gram flour to the bowl and mix. Then add the teaspoon of corn flour – this helps to bind the mixture. It should feel moist, but still fairly dry. Test the consistency by moulding a small ball of the mixture – it should hold together. Never add water to your mixture as the ingredients release their own moisture during mixing. Add a little more gram flour if the mixture seems too wet – not too much otherwise the koftas will be hard and crispy when fried.

9. Now it's time to mould the koftas ready for frying. Use the palms of your hands to mould into small balls (around 3cm by 3cm; smaller than a golf ball) – this is key for Arun, as the size helps them to cook through thoroughly. Set aside on a plate. Repeat for the rest of the mixture.

10. Check the oil is hot enough by dropping in a tiny ball of the mixture. It should rise to the top fairly quickly. Line a plate with kitchen roll, ready to receive your fried koftas.

11. Deep fry the koftas in batches over a moderate heat (too high and the outside will burn, and the inside will be uncooked). I tend to fry them in batches of 6-8, but judge according to the size of your pan. When you first drop them in, leave them to settle otherwise they may break. Arun advises only to stir once they have 'settled down' and become a pale brown colour.

12. Drain off excess oil using your slotted spoon, and remove from the oil once they have turned golden brown – the key is not to overcook them. Set aside on your lined plate.

Freeze note: once cool, freeze the koftas into sealed freezer bags.

For the tharka:
4 tablespoons rapeseed oil
1 teaspoon cumin seeds
3 cloves garlic, finely chopped
20g fresh ginger, peeled and grated
1 onion, finely chopped

1 green finger chilli, finely chopped
(or to taste)
Half teaspoon paprika
1 teaspoon salt (or to taste)
250g tomato passata
150ml single cream (some to be

used for garnish)
Around 1 cup boiling water
1 teaspoon garam masala
Fresh coriander, to garnish

For the sauce:

1. Heat the oil in a frying pan and add the cumin seeds, allowing them to sizzle.

2. Add the garlic and ginger and cook for a minute or so, followed by the onions and green chillies. Stir and allow to brown and soften.

3. Add the paprika and salt, and stir over a low heat. Cook this mixture until the onions are light brown.

4. Add the tomato passata and stir. Cook until the tharka is ready. This is when oil bubbles form around the tharka and the sauce consistency thickens.

5. Add around 100ml of the cream and stir through the tharka over a moderate heat for 2-3 minutes.

6. Add the boiling water and stir over a moderate heat. Simmer for 10 minutes uncovered, until the tharka thickens. Stir occasionally. Add the garam masala and stir.

7. Take off the heat and use a hand-blender to make a smooth tharka. Push the hand-blender right into the sauce so it doesn't splatter.

8. Just before serving, add as many koftas as you need to the tharka and serve immediately. Drizzle over the remaining cream to personal taste and garnish with coriander.

Dahi bhalle
(Lentil dumplings in yoghurt)

Dahi bhalle (also known as dahi vadas) is the name of this rich, indulgent treat, typically served as an accompaniment or starter. The word 'bhalle' refers to little dumplings made from urad and mung lentils, which are then dunked in yoghurt (dahi) and garnished with spices for a colourful finishing touch. Arun likes to serve it as a more fancy alternative to raita or plain yoghurt. Whilst Arun's family enjoy this as a side dish, some people prefer dahi bhalle as a refreshing starter, topped with tamarind and mint chutney. I have grown up eating dahi bhalle as a side dish, and I love the savoury and lightly spiced tastes, combined with the spongy texture of the dumplings.

Because the dumplings are fried, Arun only makes this dish as a treat, or for family gatherings. As with other time-consuming dishes, she makes extra bhalle and freezes them ahead. She tends to make two flavour variations, depending on her mood; one is more aligned with a traditional seasoning of cumin seeds, ginger and green chillies, and the other includes her little twist with desiccated coconut. Both are delicious, so I've given both options. The secret to this dish is getting the dumpling batter to the right consistency – thick, yet light and fluffy. It's also important to fry the dumplings until they are golden brown, so that they are crispy, but not overcooked.

Freeze note: Only the bhalle (dumplings) can be frozen. After frying, allow to cool then freeze into freezer bags. They keep well for a good month. Once thawed, follow the same method as you would after frying.

Prepare ahead: The dumplings (without the yoghurt) can be prepared a few hours in advance of serving.

Serves 7-8

To make the bhalle (dumplings):
200g urad daal (split, without skins; creamy white colour; available from any good Indian supermarket)
100g mung daal (split, without skins; pale yellow colour; available from any good Indian supermarket)

To cook:
Vegetable oil, for deep frying

To serve:
500g natural yoghurt
Half cup milk (optional)
Quarter teaspoon paprika, to garnish (or quarter teaspoon of red chilli powder if you prefer a kick)
Quarter teaspoon cumin seeds, to garnish (toast until fragrant and grind into a powder with a pestle and mortar) or quarter teaspoon garam masala
Sprig of coriander, to garnish

Flavouring option 1:
30g ginger, peeled and blended finely
2 green finger chillies (or to taste), blended finely with the ginger
1 heaped teaspoon cumin seeds
Salt, to taste

Flavouring option 2:
50g desiccated dry coconut
Handful fresh coriander, chopped (optional)
Salt, to taste

Recipe continued overleaf.

Dahi bhalle (continued)

1. Soak the lentils in warm, loose water. Cover with a lid and leave out at room temperature. The next day they will look larger and fluffier.

2. Drain through a colander.

3. Transfer the lentils to a blender, add around 100ml of water and blitz to a smooth paste. The secret is to not use too much water, otherwise the mixture becomes too runny.

4. Transfer to a large mixing bowl and add your chosen flavouring option.

5. Mix the batter vigorously until light and fluffy.

6. Leave to stand for 10 minutes. In the meantime, heat the oil for deep frying and prepare a plate lined with kitchen roll ready to receive the bhalle.

7. Test the consistency of the batter; drop a small ball of the mixture into a bowl with water. If it floats slightly, it's the right consistency. If it's too runny, Arun recommends adding just a little rice flour or semolina.

8. Once you're happy with the consistency, test that the oil is hot enough by dropping a tiny ball of the batter into the oil and seeing if it rises fairly quickly.

9. Now start frying the dumplings: carefully drop a tablespoon the batter mix into the oil for each dumpling. Add a few in one batch, but leave enough space so that they don't stick together.

10. Fry the dumplings on one side, over a moderate heat, until golden brown. (If the heat is too high, the dumplings won't cook from the inside.) After a minute or so, use a slotted spoon to gently nudge them along every now and then.

11. Once golden brown on one side, turn them over (if they haven't already turned by themselves) and cook on the other side until golden brown.

12. Remove with a slotted spoon and transfer to your lined plate. I recommend tasting the first one and spicing your batter if needed.

13. Fry until the batter is finished.

14. Now onto the soaking to get that spongy texture. For best results, this soaking should be done not long before serving so that they don't become soggy. Place the dumplings you will serve into a dish of warm water, and leave to stand for 10 minutes.

15. Use the palms of your hands to gently squeeze the excess water out of each dumpling. They should feel soft and spongy but still firm.

16. Leave the dumplings to cool on a plate.

17. In the meantime, beat the yoghurt until it's smooth and runny. Add a bit of milk at this stage to make the yoghurt a little runnier. The dumplings need to have a smooth and light yoghurt coating, which is why a slightly runny consistency works best.

18. Transfer the cooled dumplings to your serving dish and pour the yoghurt over them so that they are fully coated. For best presentation, ensure the tops of the dumplings are proudly visible in the yoghurt.

19. Garnish with spices and coriander. Serve cold.

Sheila

aloo parathas
cheeky cheese pakoras
aloo methi
arvi bhengan
karele
mint chutney
ghiya yoghurt

Treat your elders with
the same respect and
kindness that you
would like to be
shown. Good karma
comes to those who
give with genuine love.

To her six-year-old granddaughter, Sheila is a happy-go-lucky, cheerful and fun nanima. It's so easy to warm to her, with her kind eyes, beautiful laugh, and open friendly smile.

A doting mother, wife, and grandmother, Sheila loves to spend quality time with her family. Although she works six days a week in the family business, she still makes time to cook fresh Indian food most days – including 'desi' (traditionally Indian) packed lunches! Having always been close to her older sister and mum, enjoying girly chit-chat, Sheila now misses pampering her daughter, and treasures the time she spends with her granddaughter. As her daughter lives several hours away, it's a real treat when Sheila, her daughter and granddaughter unite as three generations.

Born and raised in the Punjab (Northern India), Sheila enjoyed a carefree life as the youngest of eight siblings. She was showered with love and exempt from household responsibilities when she was studying. She admits her greatest pleasures involved running around and getting up to mischief. She would create theatrical little squabbles amongst her siblings for her own entertainment. It was only when her older sister got married that young Sheila stepped up in helping around the house. Her mum had her hands full cooking fresh food three times a day – there was no fridge in the house in those days! Disapproving of her father's drinking, Sheila would turn her nose up and refuse to serve him her mum's delicious cooking unless he put the alcohol aside. Sheila has fond memories of her mum's crispy, fragrant bhindi (okra masala): "Older women just know how to make everything delicious – mum always made it look so easy!"

In her late teens, Sheila enjoyed her time as a university student. In 1980, at the age of 21, during her final year exams, she received an appealing marriage proposal from an Indian man living in the UK. Sheila left university very close to completion, and went along with the wishes of her husband and family. She got married, and moved from India to the UK.

After just a few days of settling into life in the UK, Sheila learnt just how good a man she had married, and in the most unexpected manner too. Unaware of Sheila's limited exposure to cooking, Sheila's husband Roshan was an experienced cook who had learnt from his mum. He asked Sheila to rustle up dinner for his brother and sister-in-law. Although Sheila had never cooked herself, she knew the basic skills and key ingredients from watching her mum. She realised that basic utensils and ingredients were missing from her new kitchen. Her mum always used fresh tomatoes and she sifted her flour before making atta (chapatti dough). There were no tomatoes or sieve in her new kitchen. Not one to refuse a challenge, Sheila gave the cooking a whirl and made aloo mattar (potato and peas) with chapattis. Swept up by the excitement of cooking for the first time, she threw in her onions, sprinkled in all the spices she could find, tossed in the potatoes and peas, and voilà!

Her kind brother-in-law and sister-in-law, finding her attempt endearing, sang her praises endlessly. When they left, Roshan gently told her that the dish was not well-cooked to his family's standards, and that she should throw it away. The next day, Roshan whisked Sheila off to the shops, kitted out the kitchen with every ingredient and utensil that she would need, and then spent some time teaching her the culinary techniques he had learnt from his mother and sister-in-law. He showed Sheila how to make a good tharka, the masala base for most Indian dishes, then a subji (vegetable dish), and also how to make perfect parathas. He was a confident cook.

This gift was not an act of complete selflessness though! He was rewarded from that day forward with a range of Sheila's delicious dishes. Creative Sheila built on the basics she had learnt from Roshan (and her sister-in-law), adding her own magic touches as she grew in confidence. Today, her renowned parathas (stuffed flatbreads) get her diners' mouths salivating! They are perfect in size, thickness and taste.

As thoughts then turned to starting a family, Sheila's business-minded husband bought a shop. Even though Sheila had never worked in India, she was an intelligent girl, fresh out of student life, and very eager to help her husband establish his business. Sheila would prepare aloo parathas (potato filled parathas) in the morning for breakfast, which Roshan loved. Just as porridge is fuel for the day in the western world, so were aloo parathas in India for the men who went to work the fields. Cooking hearty parathas was Sheila's way of making sure her husband was nourished and full for a day of hard work.

Sheila's next job was at a sewing factory, where she spent three years, but she did not enjoy this half as much as being in business with her husband. Sheila laughs as she describes having the Sunday night blues because her arms always hurt from working the sewing machines. This made her miss the more pampered lifestyle that she once enjoyed in India. Sheila said that when she felt homesick or lonely, she would cry at night, and then wake up ready to carry on all smiling. Apart from her day job, Sheila also became a carer to her ill mother-in-law, who needed attention during the night. Sheila wouldn't have it any other way though. She cherished her relationship with her mother-in-law, and to this day feels grateful for the blessings she received from her. Her mother-in-law would shower her with kindness and affectionately call her 'Sheiloh', reminding her of the love she grew up with in India. As a doting daughter-in-law, Sheila presented her first pay cheque of £22 (for five days' work) to her mother-in-law, out of respect. Sweetly, her kind mother-in-law closed her hands and returned the money, telling her to buy herself something.

Sheila liked the fact that she was able to help her husband pay the bills. Even after giving birth to her daughter, Sheila went straight back to work at the sewing factory, knowing that her young family would need the extra money. In the meantime, her strategic husband was planning new business moves, and opened a bag shop, which meant moving house. Sheila used this opportunity to go into business with her husband again, and she enjoyed being her own boss rather than working in the sewing factory.

Sheila is proactive but laid-back in her approach to life; the most important thing to her is that her son, daughter and granddaughter are happy and healthy in their lives. But there's nothing which pleases Sheila more than cooking for guests, especially when her granddaughter lovingly asks: "Nanima, can we have a cheese pakora party?!"

Sheila shares one piece of advice which she holds close to her heart – it's the advice she was given by her parents, and is based on her positive relationships with her elders. She advises to respect one's elders with genuine kindness – the blessings you receive from them are invaluable. Her particular example is in relation to her in-laws. Sheila was advised by her own mother to treat one's in-laws with the same kindness and respect as you would give your own parents. To give some context, to show respect for one's elders, and receive blessings in return, is embedded in the Indian culture (this is how I was raised). It is a customary greeting in some families, including my own and Sheila's, to bow and touch the feet of significant elders, which is then returned with a series of kind blessings.

Sheila is happiest when she is cooking, entertaining guests and playing with her granddaughter. Sheila is young at heart, and this really shone through in our conversations – you can talk about anything with her and she's a great advisor.

"Just as porridge is fuel for the day in the western world, so were aloo parathas in India for the men who went to work the fields."

Aloo parathas

I have already written about the magic of Sheila's aloo parathas (potato stuffed flatbreads) in her story, but having sampled them for myself, I experienced how addictive they are, and how easy it is to have another. These parathas are the perfect treat for Sunday brunch, or breakfast in a group gathering. I joined Sheila and her family for Sunday breakfast when watching her cook these. They are the best that I've ever tried! I am delighted to share this recipe with you so that you can also enjoy them.

Like rotis, parathas take a lot of practice. Many dadimas, and women I know, take great pride in their parathas and it's taken years to perfect that skill. This is one of those dishes where even a detailed recipe cannot replace practice. Experienced cooks like Sheila make it look effortless preparing parathas, whilst casually flipping the other on the chapatti pan. But don't be put-off! If you are new to making parathas, work out a little production line so that you can have one paratha at the ready whilst the other is cooking. Sheila's top tips are as follows: the stuffing must be flavoursome, so make sure you taste it. Roll out the parathas as evenly as possible, but try not to overdo it with the flour (other than when specified to coat in flour) – this is an art! Too much flour can create burnt marks on the surface. Make sure your frying pan is hot before cooking. Keep the heat moderate throughout, to prevent burning. Only add oil to the parathas once it has cooked on both sides, and don't add too much.

Making parathas can be quite messy, so even if you don't plan on eating them all in one sitting, it's worth making them at once to avoid further mess. The parathas can keep in a cool, dry place for the next day, or alternatively you can freeze them. The dough for rotis and parathas is the same, so to make life easier, I refer you to Kamla's roti recipe for the dough-making part.

Since parathas are slow releasers of energy, quite heavy, and keep you full for some time, they are traditionally enjoyed in the morning. It's also not uncommon in India for people to indulge in a few parathas, and then have a little afternoon snooze. For a simple, tasty meal, serve parathas with a bowl of natural yoghurt and a spoon of achar (pickle). Without further ado, I leave you to plan your own paratha party!

Prepare ahead: Make the dough and the mixture up to a day in advance and store in the fridge.

Freeze note: Once cool, freeze the parathas in sheets of greaseproof paper, then seal well in clingfilm. Thaw and re-heat in a frying pan.

Makes 5 parathas

You will need: *Tongs to flip the parathas, a rolling pin and a flat chapatti pan (tawa), a dough mixer if you don't want to knead by hand.*

For the dough:
See pages 211- 212, Kamla's rotis recipe. Use the same quantities for the dough and follow steps under 'preparing the atta'.

For the aloo stuffing:
2 medium-sized white potatoes (or potatoes equating to just under 300g)
Half an onion, very finely chopped
1 green finger chilli, finely chopped (or to taste)
Half teaspoon ajawain (carom seeds)
Half teaspoon salt (or to taste)
Half teaspoon paprika
Half teaspoon garam masala
Half teaspoon amchoor (mango powder)
Handful coriander (or fenugreek leaves), chopped
Rapeseed oil, to cook

Recipe continued overleaf.

Aloo parathas (continued)

1. Boil the potatoes until soft enough to mash. When cool enough to handle, peel and transfer to a mixing bowl.
2. Mash the potatoes roughly so that there are still small chunks.
3. Add the chopped onions, all of the spices and the coriander. Mix well.
4. Taste your mixture and add more spices if necessary.
5. Start heating your pan over a low heat whilst you make the parathas. It's really important to have a hot pan so that the parathas cooks all the way through.

Once you're ready to make your parathas, clear and prepare your workstation. You need a clean, dry surface with plenty of room to roll the dough – ideally next to your cooker. Keep your flour for coating in a wide bowl, and a bowl of oil (around 7 tablespoons) for cooking the parathas. You'll also need something to put the parathas on as they come off the heat – either an insulated container, or a plate lined with kitchen roll.

6. Divide your dough into 5 equal pieces, weighing approximately 100g each.
7. Take the first piece and roll between the palms of your hands to form a round ball shape. Lightly toss in the bowl of loose flour.
8. Flatten the dough ball, rotating against the palm of your hands as you do so. Roll out a small circle of around 5 inches in diameter.
9. Now to fill the parathas. Place around 2 heaped tablespoons of mixture in the centre of the dough.
10. Gently pull up the sides of the dough, making it into a little parcel which seals at the top. You should feel some excess dough between your fingers – twist this around and then push it back into the dough as if it were a button sealing the dough.
11. Flatten the dough ball against the work surface, then lightly coat with the flour.
12. Roll the parathas into a circle shape of around 8 inches in diameter: carefully roll a few times in one direction, then flip the parathas, and roll a few times in another direction. If necessary, very lightly flour to prevent sticking.
13. Clap between your hands then place on the hot chapatti pan. Cook for 1 to 1 and a half minutes on one side. You will notice a change in the surface colour.
14. Flip over and heat the other side for 1 to 1 and a half minutes.
15. Drizzle and spread just over 1 teaspoon of oil over the surface of the paratha. Make sure you get to the edges.
16. Flip over and spread oil as above.
17. Continue to heat the paratha over a moderate heat, flipping only once or twice, until it is golden brown and crispy.
18. Repeat to make the remaining parathas.
19. Enjoy with a knob of butter (if you wish), a bowl of natural yoghurt, and a mug of masala chai.

Cheeky cheese pakoras

If you love cheese and are not precious about a little indulgence, these bread pakoras are for you. Bread pakoras, a bit like fried sandwiches, are enjoyed in some parts of India as a street food snack, or breakfast dish. Some are made with two slices of bread per pakora, but Sheila prefers to use one slice per pakora. She has always used white bread as she thinks it fries better. As they are quite filling and indulgent, Sheila only cooks them on special occasions. This is usually when her granddaughter comes to visit from London and requests a pakora tea party! She's got it right though – these pakoras make a brilliant party snack. Sheila's granddaughter feels important helping her make these – her job is to dunk the bread in water and stack up the slices. I saw the two of them bonding over this cooking stage, and their love just made me love cheese pakoras even more.

Sheila's secret tip is to wet the bread on one side, so that it can be scrunched into an improvised pakora. The most important thing is to fully seal the pakora with water and batter, so that oil doesn't seep into the pakoras when frying.

Sheila keeps the crusts on so as not to waste (as you'll see from our photoshoot, I went with her preference!). However, having experimented with crusts on and off, I can say that I'm a 'crusts off' person as I like the neat finish it gives. As it's smaller, it means slightly less mixture per pakora. I also prefer to lightly cook the onions, rather than adding them raw to the mixture, as I find it reduces that lingering sharp taste in the mouth.

If you happen to have leftover pakoras, they keep well in the fridge for around two days, and taste best re-heated in the oven. Serve with a generous helping of mint chutney (see Sheila's recipe on p160) – if you're like me you'll also add a cheeky squirt of tomato ketchup! These are not posh pakoras with fancy ingredients – they are unapologetically great comfort food for cheese and bread lovers!

Makes 14 pakoras (crusts off)
Oil, for deep frying
14 slices white bread, crusts neatly sliced off close to the edge of the bread
Bowlful of cold water
3 tablespoons rapeseed oil (to fry the onions)

For the filling:
1 red onion, finely chopped
120g mature cheddar cheese, grated
75g frozen peas, boiled and left to cool

75g frozen sweetcorn, boiled with the peas and left to cool
Quarter teaspoon paprika
Three quarter teaspoon salt (or to taste)
1 teaspoon garam masala
Half teaspoon red chilli powder (or to taste)
Half teaspoon black pepper

For the batter:
4 tablespoons gram flour (known as besan in Indian supermarkets)

Half teaspoon salt (or to taste)
Handful freshly chopped coriander (or fenugreek leaves)
Water, to mix

Prepare ahead: *Fry the onion, and boil the peas and sweetcorn a few hours in advance of cooking so that they can cool. If you wish, make the entire mixture up to a day in advance and keep refrigerated.*

Recipe continued overleaf.

147

1. Heat the oil in a frying pan and add the onions. Fry until softened then set aside and leave to cool.
2. Add all ingredients for the filling into a large mixing bowl and stir well.
3. Prepare the batter. Add the gram flour, salt and coriander to a separate bowl. Gradually add water, stirring as you do, until it becomes a liquid paste consistency.
4. Prepare your workstation. Set out a plate lined with kitchen roll to receive the fried pakoras, the bowlful of cold water, the batter, the pakora mixture and the stack of bread. Heat the oil for deep frying whilst you prepare the pakoras.
5. Pat water onto one side of each slice. Each slice should be firm and moist, not floppy and soaked. Stack same side down – the filling will go onto the wet side.
6. Check the oil is hot by dropping a tiny breadcrumb into it and checking it rises to the top quickly.
7. Take one slice of bread and place wet side up on your hand. Place a handful of mixture into the centre.
8. Gently scrunch the bread into a round, sealed parcel. Wet your hands with water as you scrunch, to help the sealing stay in place. Ensure there are no gaps.
9. Dunk the dumpling into your batter, fully coating all sides. Mould a little further into a compact shape.
10. Repeat steps 7-9 to prepare a few more pakoras so that you can fry a batch together.
11. Carefully slip the pakoras into the oil. Do this from the sides of the pan so that hot oil doesn't splash. Leave space between each pakora.
12. When the bottom half of the pakoras turn golden brown, carefully turn each one individually.
13. Allow the other side to cook until golden brown.
14. Remove from the oil once golden brown, draining off excess oil using your slotted spoon. Place on your lined plate.
15. Repeat steps to prepare and fry the remainder of your pakoras.
16. Serve hot and enjoy with a mug of masala chai.

"These are not posh pakoras with fancy ingredients – they are unapologetically great comfort food for cheese and bread lovers!"

Aloo methi

Aloo methi (potatoes with fenugreek) is a really simple and straightforward dish. I love the slightly bitter undertone and distinctive aroma. In this dish, I always opt for fresh fenugreek. If it's on offer, I often buy extra and freeze it after the blending stage.

Sheila likes to serve her aloo methi with rotis, mung daal and a yoghurt dish. Sheila's husband enjoys any leftovers the following day in toasted sandwiches! I've adapted Sheila's recipe a little, in that I prefer not to use tomatoes. I've added haldi, and I also roughly blend the methi. I cook my aloo methi in a shallow, heavy-based frying pan with a lid.

Serves 4-5 as a side dish
3 bunches fresh fenugreek leaves
(methi)
5 tablespoons rapeseed oil
1 teaspoon cumin seeds (jeera)
1 large white onion, finely chopped
20g ginger, peeled and grated
3 cloves garlic, finely chopped
2 green finger chillies, finely chopped
(or to taste)
1 teaspoon salt (or to taste)

Half teaspoon turmeric powder
(haldi)
4 medium-sized white potatoes (or
potatoes equating to around 600g),
peeled and chopped into chunks of
around 1 inch
Half teaspoon garam masala

Prepare ahead: *Prepare the methi*
a few hours ahead of cooking.

1. First prepare the methi. Remove the leaves from the stalks, wash thoroughly, then leave to dry in a colander.
2. Roughly blend the methi until it looks finely chopped. Set aside.
3. Heat the oil in a heavy-based frying pan, add the cumin seeds and allow to sizzle.
4. Add the onions and cook until light brown, stirring regularly.
5. Stir in the ginger, garlic and chillies and cook for around 4-5 minutes over a moderate heat.
6. Add the salt and haldi and stir well.
7. Add the potato chunks, and coat fully in the onion masala. Add a dash of boiling water before simmering, as this will prevent the potatoes from burning.
8. Simmer the potatoes, covered, on a low heat until half-cooked. Stir occasionally.
9. Stir through the methi. Simmer, covered, until the potatoes are soft enough to be pierced with a knife, but not mushy.
10. Stir through the garam masala and serve hot.

Arvi bhengan
(Taro root and aubergines)

Arvi is the Punjabi word for taro root, the vegetable which grows from the tropical taro plant – supposedly one of the oldest known crops. If you've not cooked with it before, it's used in a similar way to potato, and has been used for years as a staple ingredient in various world cuisines. It can be found in Indian supermarkets under the name of arbi or arvi. Because there are several varieties of taro, which look similar in appearance, shopping for them can be a little confusing. For this dish, Sheila and the dadimas I know have always cooked with the small, brown and hairy taro root (arvi) which are crookedly shaped (see photo), rather than the larger vegetable which has a ringed effect on the surface.

Arvi bhengan is a hidden gem, which in my opinion isn't celebrated enough in mainstream Indian cooking. It's one of Sheila's treasured dishes. Sheila deep fries the taro root, but I prefer to oven-cook it. The vegetable is known to contain calcium oxalate, so it must not be eaten in its raw state and care must be taken to ensure it is cooked through thoroughly. For the same reason, handling raw taro root can cause itchiness in the hands. Sheila oils her hands before handling it, but I always wear gloves as I have sensitive skin.

Sheila loves to use the long, slim baby aubergines, as these smaller ones look quite the delicacy when served. You can also use the round, baby aubergines (known as Indian eggplants), as photographed. Cook the aubergines whole, but create an opening by slicing each one into quarters, and not taking the knife right through the top of the aubergine. It tastes great with daal, rotis and ghiya yoghurt.

Serves 4-5 as a side dish

6 pieces arvi (taro root), or equating to around 250g arvi

6 tablespoons rapeseed oil (for cooking and for roasting the arvi)

1 teaspoon cumin seeds

1 onion, finely chopped

3 cloves fresh garlic, finely chopped

30g ginger, peeled and grated

2 green finger chillies, finely chopped (or to taste)

1 teaspoon turmeric powder (haldi)

Quarter teaspoon paprika

Three quarter teaspoon salt (or to taste)

200g tomato passata

5 baby aubergines (or equating to around 300g), left whole but sliced almost to the top into quarters

1 level teaspoon garam masala

1 level teaspoon cinnamon powder

Recipe continued overleaf.

Arvi bhengan (continued)

1. Pre-heat your oven to 180°C. Using a potato peeler, remove the hairy skin from the arvi. Chop into quarters and wash thoroughly in cold water. Lightly pat dry with kitchen roll.

2. Drizzle some of the oil over the arvi pieces and oven cook for 25-30 minutes. Cook until soft enough to pierce with a knife, but not mushy. You'll need to remember to turn them halfway through cooking. Whilst the arvi is cooking, make the tharka (onion masala base).

3. Heat around 4 tablespoons of the oil in a wide, heavy-based pan. Add the cumin seeds, allow to sizzle and then stir in the onions.

4. Cook until the onions are light brown, stirring regularly. Then add the garlic, ginger and green chillies and stir well.

5. Stir in the haldi, paprika and salt.

6. Stir in the tomato passata and cook for 2 minutes over a medium heat.

7. Add around half a cup of boiling water. This loosens the consistency of the tharka so that it seeps into the aubergines.

8. Add the aubergines and stir the tharka into the sliced openings.

9. Cover and simmer for 10 minutes until the tharka thickens and the aubergines soften slightly. Stir occasionally, and if necessary add a little more boiling water to prevent sticking.

10. Add the cooked arvi to the pan and stir through.

11. Cover and simmer for a further 5-10 minutes.

12. Stir through the garam masala and cinnamon powder and serve hot.

"If you've not cooked with it before, it's used in a similar way to potato, and has been used for years as a staple ingredient in various world cuisines. It can be found in Indian supermarkets under the name of arbi or arvi."

Karele

Karele*, an interesting vegetable (technically a fruit) known as bitter gourd, belongs to the same plant family as watermelon, cucumber and pumpkin. If you've never tried karele before, it's a lot like Marmite – you either love it or hate it! True to its name, it has a slightly bitter taste, which is mellowed with the right cooking conditions.

Don't be put off by its rather intimidating spiky appearance! The spikiness is peeled off in this recipe, and once cooked thoroughly, it softens up nicely. I've even managed to impress guests who don't usually eat karele, including my father!

The secret is to balance the bitter taste with the right amount of sweet and sour flavouring. I've made a few tweaks based on tips I've learnt from watching other dadimas. Whilst Sheila adds cinnamon powder at the end, I use brown sugar and mango powder in the recipe overleaf. I also peel the karele and leave them in lemon juice and salt before cooking. Instead of deep frying, I prefer to shallow fry.

When Sheila taught me her version of karele, her husband was also on hand to help out and offer his words of wisdom. He spoke proudly and excitedly about karele. Being diabetic, he knew all too well about its supposed benefits for diabetes sufferers and enlightened me to the fact that they have been used in herbal remedies for generations.

If you've never made karele before, start off with a small quantity – three or four fruits. It's more of an accompaniment than a main dish, and because of its bold flavour and acquired taste, it is best enjoyed in small portions. Serve karele with milder flavours which won't overpower its taste – mung daal, a yoghurt dish, and a few rotis make a great combo.

Prepare ahead: See steps 1 and 2 (overleaf).

* Karele is plural and karela refers to one fruit.

See the karele recipe overleaf.

Karele (continued)

Serves 4 as a side dish
3 karele (bitter gourds)
Juice of half a lemon
1 and a half teaspoons salt (or to taste)
Vegetable oil for shallow frying, plus 2 tablespoons oil for cooking
1 teaspoon cumin seeds

1 onion, sliced to medium thickness
3 cloves garlic, finely chopped
20g ginger, peeled and grated
2 green finger chillies, finely chopped (or to taste)
1 teaspoon turmeric powder (haldi)
Half teaspoon mango powder (amchoor)

1 teaspoon brown sugar
120g plum tomatoes, blended
Three quarter teaspoon garam masala

1. Lightly peel off the spiky parts of the karele skin using a potato peeler (exert just enough pressure to take off the spikes). Slice each karela through the middle. Use a teaspoon or knife to scoop out the seeds and flesh. Slice each half down the centre. Cut into strips of approximately 2 inches and transfer to a bowl.

2. Add the lemon juice and around 1 teaspoon of salt to the bowl. Stir well. Cover with clingfilm and refrigerate for 2-3 hours, or overnight if you have time.

3. Heat the oil for shallow frying. Add the karele and cook for 10-15 minutes over a medium heat, stirring regularly. They should be slightly crispy, but easily pierced with a knife. Once cooked, transfer to a plate and set aside whilst you make the tharka (onion masala base).

4. In the same frying pan, heat 2 tablespoons of oil if needed (depending on amount of grease left). Add the cumin seeds, allow to sizzle, then stir in the onions.

5. Cook the onions until light brown, stirring regularly.

6. Add the garlic, ginger and green chillies and cook for 1 minute.

7. Stir through the haldi, mango powder, remaining salt, and brown sugar. Cook until the onions are medium brown, stirring regularly.

8. Add the tomatoes and stir until the tharka is ready. This is when the consistency thickens and oil bubbles form around the mixture.

9. Stir through the cooked karele. Cover and simmer for 5 minutes.

10. Stir through garam masala and serve hot.

"Don't be put off by its rather intimidating spiky appearance! The spikiness is peeled off in this recipe, and once cooked thoroughly, it softens up nicely. I've even managed to impress guests who don't usually eat karele, including my father!"

Mint chutney

Sheila's family love her mint chutney, and she always makes extra to share with family and friends. It's a perfect accompaniment to many summer dishes, particularly barbecue food, salads and toasted panini sandwiches. In the winter, it makes a vivacious accompaniment to lamb dishes and roast dinners. Sheila loves eating it with samosas and pakoras, but her favourite way to enjoy it is with fresh rotis straight off the tawa and yellow mung daal. Like Sheila, I also like to make extra chutney to share with friends and family. It's a super easy chutney to make, but because of the preparation involved, it makes sense to make a batch of it. It stays fresh in the fridge for a good seven days. I've even frozen it and it still tasted great.

Sheila adds a squirt of tomato ketchup and hot pepper sauce to her chutney. I've played around with different combinations, and have instead chosen to add brown sugar, mango powder, and a pinch of garam masala. A dash of fresh imlee (tamarind) chutney is also one of the options I've explored, as it adds a brilliant bittersweet flavour (see the recipe for Indu's imlee chutney on p176). Sheila uses equal amounts of coriander and mint, but I prefer using more mint to emphasise its unique flavour.

Some people like the mild and cooling flavour of yoghurt mint chutney. If you do, simply add some natural yoghurt to the mint chutney, so that it becomes a separate chutney.

Makes around 15-20 servings
Small handful coriander leaves, washed and left to dry
2 bunches mint leaves, washed and left to dry
1 red onion
1 white onion
2 fresh salad tomatoes
1 teaspoon mango powder (amchoor)

1 teaspoon salt (or to taste)
2 heaped teaspoons brown sugar (or to taste)
2 tablespoons tamarind chutney (optional)
2 green finger chillies (or to taste)
Half teaspoon garam masala (optional)
Half cup to 1 cup of water, to be added gradually

You will need: *A good blender.*

Prepare ahead note: *Pick the coriander and mint leaves so that any large stalks are removed. Dice the onions and cut the tomatoes ready for the blender.*

1. Throw all of the ingredients into a good blender with a splash of water and give it a whizz.
2. Taste the chutney and add more of each ingredient according to personal taste. I usually taste for salt and sweetness.
3. Blitz again until it reaches a really smooth consistency. If you find that all of the ingredients are not blending smoothly, add half a cup of water. Always start with less and add more as you see fit.
4. Serve cold as a zingy accompaniment.

Ghiya yoghurt

Ghiya refers to the smooth, light green bottle gourd (see inset picture below). Ghiya yoghurt is best described, in the opinion of Sheila and the other dadimas I know, as the upmarket version of cucumber raita. I know for a fact that ghiya yoghurt was my grandfather's favourite accompaniment, and it's also Sheila's husband's favourite. Cucumber raita is a well-known yoghurt dish, but this version with ghiya is an understated classic – often spoken about with an approving smile by the dadimas I've met.

There are several varieties which come in different shapes and sizes. In Indian supermarkets, you'll find it under the names of 'dhudi', 'lauki' or 'ghiya', and there is usually a round one and a long bottle one. Out of the two, I always buy the long bottle-shaped one, but you can buy any. It's a surprisingly versatile vegetable – other dadimas in this book have taught me to use ghiya in koftas and in certain lentil dishes.

You can serve ghiya yoghurt with most main dishes – I've grown up with yoghurt as a star side dish with all Indian meals. The delicate crunch and subtle taste of ghiya makes it a perfect match for Greek yoghurt, which Sheila always uses for this side. I prefer to use half natural yoghurt mixed with half Greek yoghurt. Bottle gourd itself is deceivingly easy to prepare. For this recipe, we simply peel and grate it, then boil and squeeze out the water. Squeezing out the water is a great step to get the kids involved in – Sheila's granddaughter feels very important doing this job!

Prepare ahead: Prepare the yoghurt up to a day in advance and refrigerate. Garnish and add salt just before serving (optional).

Serves 4-5
1 long bottle gourd (ghiya)
200g Greek yoghurt
200g natural yoghurt
Salt, to taste

Small handful of pomegranate seeds
to garnish
Pinch of garam masala and paprika,
to garnish (optional)

1. Wash, peel and grate the ghiya.
2. Transfer to a saucepan and boil in loose water. Once the water has boiled, simmer for 20-30 minutes until the ghiya is soft.
3. In the meantime, mix the natural and Greek yoghurt in a bowl until smooth.
4. Drain the ghiya through a fine sieve and rinse through cold water until cool enough to handle.
5. Take a handful of ghiya and use your hands to squeeze out all excess water. Repeat until you have done this for all of the ghiya.
6. Mix the ghiya through the yoghurt and add salt to taste.
7. Garnish with the pomegranate, paprika and garam masala.

Indu

jeera chicken wings
karah
tamarind chutney
aloo papdi chaat
paneer with peppers
mushroom subji
spring lamb

I ndu is one of the younger dadimas in this book. Looking at her, you would never think that she was mother to four children, and dadima to two grandchildren (at the time of writing).

As modern, effortlessly glamorous, and busy as she is, Indu makes time for traditional Indian cooking and holds onto the classic home values she was taught. Indu enjoys family gatherings, cooking for others and entertaining. Growing up in West London, with busy parents and a large immediate family, Indu learnt how to quickly put a meal on the table by creatively cooking with her older sister. When her parents were working late, the two elder sisters would rustle up food for their siblings through teamwork. Whether it tasted delicious, or looked amazing, was another matter!

Post-marriage, cooking took on a whole new ball game for Indu, where her philosophy on food and home-building was shaped by a very special woman. In the 1980s, during her teens, 16-year-old Indu married into a large extended family and spent a lot of time with a strong, highly talented, and loving matriarch. Indeed, it was Indu's mother-in-law who passed down her culinary and domestic wisdom.

Indu's mother-in-law (she's affectionately known as 'mummah', meaning mum) taught her the value of eating breakfast and evening meals together as a family. A family that eats together, stays together! Early on in marriage, Indu learnt the importance of putting a meal on the table for her husband who worked long hours. A successful marriage went hand-in-hand with her preparing nourishing food. As the saying goes, the way to a man's heart is through his stomach!

Indu's mother-in-law was not only a fine cook and homemaker, but also a qualified seamstress. She lovingly created unique pieces for her dear children and grandchildren as a hobby. Indu was a keen apprentice, and as a young bride she learnt a lot from her mother-in-law. Having seen Indu's obsessive cleanliness in the kitchen, her smooth multi-tasking, and very fussy cooking rituals, it's evident that the teachings of 'mummah' are embedded in her cooking approach.

Indu's mother-in-law taught her gradually with love and support. It was a good job that she took this approach, as a few months after marriage Indu fell pregnant with her first child, and very quickly she learnt the reality of multi-tasking!

Initially (when she wasn't suffering from morning sickness), young Indu took on the role of apprentice chef: chopping ingredients, watching and learning, cleaning, and connecting with her mother-in-law over food and conversation. One of the most important culinary secrets Indu learnt, and still lives by, is this: "Once you've mastered a good tharka (the onion masala base to a dish), you've got the tools to make most dishes." Indu would observe her mother-in-law carefully, paying real attention to how spices were used in each dish. She would memorise the dishes and then cook them herself, trying to emulate her mother-in-law's style. As Indu grew in confidence, her mother-in-law took more of a back seat, giving Indu the space to cook alone. Not only did Indu learn how to cook a feast for entertaining, but her culinary repertoire also extended to all-time classic dishes, including those cooked during Hindu festivals (for example, the sacred semolina pudding 'karah' – in this chapter). Before too long, Indu was entrusted with the daily ritual of preparing Indian lunch for those who work in the family business. She would repeatedly practice her mother-in-law's dishes, sometimes burning the food during the early days, then throwing it away and starting all over again! Practice makes perfect, she was taught. Back then, batch cooking, or using leftovers, was completely out of the question! Fresh food was cooked on a daily basis. Nowadays, taking shortcuts and batch-cooking has become part of our lives. When Indu was young, she didn't use electric dough-makers to make chapatti flour, for example.

Indu shared what her mother-in-law did in India and Kenya, in relation to preparing a typically balanced meal. It consisted of one subji (a vegetarian dish), one meat dish (the men in the family were big on meat!), one lentil dish, a salad, home-made yoghurt, and freshly-made chapattis. Indu stressed what an amazing cook her mother-in-law was, and still is – she is even able to judge the taste and flavour of the meat dishes she cooks, despite having been vegetarian her whole life!

By the age of 21, Indu had been married five years, and was mother to three children. She was no longer living with her mother-in-law, but neighbour to her! Indu was so used to cooking within the extended family that it became second nature to cook a large quantity and send some food over to share next door. Indu and her mother-in-law would let each other know when they had cooked a meat or a lentil dish, to avoid duplication and help each other out. When I heard this part of her story, I thought, 'now that's resourceful cooking and teamwork!'

When Indu moved home, she took her mother-in-law's masala dabba (spice storage tub) with her as a sentimental keepsake. To this day, Indu still uses it and talks nostalgically about how she learnt to cook using this very dabba. Domestic goddess, dutiful daughter-in-law, brilliant mum and wife – Indu juggled her roles skilfully (although she's too humble to put it that way!). Looking back, Indu realises just how busy those years were as a multitasking mother. Now that she's also a dadima, Indu feels fortunate to spend quality time with her grandchildren.

By the time Indu's children had grown up, she had only just begun to come to terms with her role as a mother. She felt in no way ready to become a mother-in-law, or dadima! But when her son got married, Indu had a mental checklist of how to welcome her daughter-in-law who was to live with her for a short while. She would wake up bright and early, always prepare a heart-warming meal, and be there for the new couple, whilst also giving them space.

Indu rightly points out that times have changed, and that she could not take the same approach as her mother-in-law today. She appreciates how more women are choosing to focus their attention on their careers and education, and as a result, marry later in life. She is very supportive of this. Indu and her mother-in-law have built a special bond over years of home-cooking and shared responsibilities. To this day, Indu is doted upon by her mother-in-law, and food is still central to their conversations. Cooking together was not just about preparing food – it built the foundation of their relationship as daughter-in-law and mother-in-law. They connected over shared values, like the importance of enjoying meals together as a family, food as fuel and nourishment for the day, and preparing food with love and care for the family.

Apart from her culinary wisdom, which is vast, Indu shares a few pieces of life advice with me, which she wants to pass onto her children and grandchildren. A lesson passed down to her from her mum is to always think carefully before speaking, so that you do not regret what you've said afterwards. At the same time, she says: "Never think that you are too big a person to apologise". Onto marriage, the advice that Indu would give to her daughters is this: "As educated and career-driven modern women may be, there is also invaluable worth in having a good understanding of cooking and making a home". Indu stresses the importance of simple, traditional family values, particularly those of being there for one another, building strong family bonds, and eating dinner together.

Sure enough, Indu's husband Suneel is full of praise and admiration for her. In fact, he says that he cannot tell the difference between his mother's cooking and Indu's! Without further ado, I'll leave you to experiment with Indu's delicious dishes, paying particular attention to her wise words that the tharka is the number one priority!

"Once you've mastered a good tharka (the onion masala base to a dish), you've got the tools to make most dishes."

SIGNATURE DISH:

Jeera chicken wings

Indu's jeera (cumin) chicken wings are her husband's favourite, and a real hit at her dinner parties. An experienced Indu stresses just how easy they are to cook. However, there is a knack to achieving well-flavoured wings with a dry but succulent texture. Indu's secret is to get the right balance of herbs and spices and to simmer. She stirs her wings frequently and will only leave the cooker unattended once they are at the simmering stage. Indu always cooks this dish in a stainless steel karahi and I would recommend doing so (or using a heavy-based, bowl-shaped frying pan).

Indu prefers to use the drumette of the chicken wing (out of the flat, drumette and tip), and always use a skinless meat. Don't worry if you can only get hold of the full wing joints. For each wing, remove the tip, then cut at the joint to use the drumette and flat.

This dish makes a perfect starter alongside aloo tikkis (see Bholi's recipe on p68), a chutney and a salad.

Serves 6

5 tablespoons rapeseed oil
5-6 teaspoons cumin seeds (jeera)
1 small white onion, finely blended
4 cloves garlic
25g ginger, peeled and blended with the garlic
1 teaspoon salt (or to taste)
Half teaspoon red chilli powder (or to taste)
1 heaped teaspoon paprika
1 heaped teaspoon garam masala
3 green finger chillies, topped and snapped in half (or to taste)
1kg skinless chicken wing drumettes
Handful fresh fenugreek leaves (methi), finely chopped (or 1 and half tablespoons dried fenugreek – sold as kasuri methi in Indian supermarkets)
Three quarter teaspoon ground black pepper
Half cup – 1 cup of boiling water
Handful fresh coriander, finely chopped

1. Heat the oil in a karahi then add the cumin seeds. Stir over a medium heat until fragrant and sizzling.
2. Stir in the onions and cook until they begin to soften.
3. Add the garlic and ginger. Cook until the onions are medium brown.
4. Stir through the spices and green chillies. Cook for 1 minute.
5. Stir in the chicken wings over a medium heat, ensuring they are fully coated with the onion masala.
6. Add the fenugreek and black pepper. Stir. Add half a cup to 1 cup of boiling water (enough to half cover the wings) before simmering.
7. Cover and simmer the chicken wings for 45 minutes on a low heat. Check once or twice and stir.
8. Garnish with coriander and serve hot.

Karah
(Semolina pudding)

Karah (semolina pudding) is a sacred dish in the Sikh and Hindu communities. Hot, smooth and sweet, it's like a hug in a bowl. It's one of those 'every now and then' treats to look forward to as a dessert, or enjoy with an afternoon cuppa. The great thing is that it doesn't take long to make, and you can keep it in the fridge for a couple of days. Like roti and rice, there are just a few simple ingredients, but there is an art to putting them together – and Indu has mastered that art to perfection. Try this recipe when you're in the mood for stirring – it takes some elbow grease!

I cannot share such a powerfully symbolic dish without any context. Following Hindu customs passed down to her by her mother-in-law, Indu makes karah to mark the end of a religious festival (called Navratri), which celebrates the different qualities of a Hindu goddess. Indu prepares karah along with puris (deep fried bread) and glossy black chickpeas, in a dry-roasted tharka. Traditionally, the chickpeas and karah are placed inside the puri, with a £1 coin placed on top, as a gift for young girls. The Hindu celebration honours young girls, as they are believed to symbolise purity and innocence. I have fond memories – both from childhood and more recently – of tucking into my little parcel of karah puris. When I'm feeling nostalgic and in need of a wholesome dessert, I cook karah by itself.

Indu is known as the karah puri queen in her family! Whilst I learnt the full karah puri recipe (at 5am!) from Indu, it is quite fiddly and time-consuming, and the dishes tend to be cooked on a large scale. Here, I share with you the recipe for the karah, or semolina pudding, which tastes delicious eaten on its own.

Depending on how much you want to make, use the same measuring tool for consistency – Indu likes to measure with cups. I use my little 175ml teacup, which makes around 6-8 small servings – I enjoy karah in small quantities as it is a treat dish.

The key to this dish is being precise with your ratios and looking out for key tell-tale signs during the cooking process. Indu uses a ratio of 1 cup of semolina, to 1 and a half cups of sugar, to 3 cups of water. If you like real sweetness, go with Indu's ratio. In the recipe below, however, I've tweaked the ratio to my personal taste, which has less sugar. I use 1 cup of semolina, to just under 1 cup of sugar, to 2 cups of water.

Indu's secret to judging when the semolina is cooked is when you start to smell the aroma and it fills the room. It's crucial to keep stirring this dish, and pressing down on the semolina so that there are no lumps. Cook over a moderate heat so that the semolina doesn't burn. Indu's optimum semolina colour is a glazed, light golden brown. You'll be able to tell the colour of your end product once the semolina and butter have mixed. It should not turn dark brown, as this means that it has burnt. You can also tell when the semolina is cooked once you see little bubbles of butter separating from the semolina around the edges of the pan. When you're stirring all the ingredients together, you'll know when the karah is done when it slides effortlessly around the pan. These secret tips were passed down to Indu by her mother-in-law.

Indu prefers to use a stainless steel karahi for this dish, and I do too. If you don't have one, just use a wide, heavy-based pan, preferably with a rounded base. You don't need to garnish karah if you don't want to. I've used saffron in the photo because my family had some at home after our travels to the Middle East. A couple of crushed green cardamoms do the trick just as well.

Store note: Karah keeps for a few days in an airtight container. To serve, re-heat in the microwave to a warm temperature.

See the karah recipe overleaf.

Karah (continued)

Serves 6-8
75g unsalted butter
150g white sugar
350ml cold water
110g fine semolina

Pinch saffron, to garnish and stir
through (optional)
Seeds of 2 green cardamom pods, to
garnish (optional)

1. Melt the butter in a heavy-based pan over a low heat.

2. In a separate saucepan, heat the sugar and water over a low heat. This will form a sugar syrup to be added later.

3. Stir the semolina into the butter until it has a texture like breadcrumbs.

4. Push down on the lumps of semolina, using the back of your spoon, until the mixture is smooth and light golden brown. Indu stresses that the heat must be fairly low to prevent the semolina from burning and turning dark brown.

5. Stir constantly until the semolina is cooked. This is when it is aromatic and smooth in consistency. Small bubbles of butter will be released around the mixture. Only once the mixture has reached this point, should the sugar syrup be added.

6. Stir the sugar syrup to ensure the granules have dissolved, then carefully pour it into the semolina.

7. Stir the karah continuously over a low heat. The consistency will thicken almost immediately. Stir until it comes together as one dollop and is sliding around the pan without sticking.

8. As soon as it reaches this stage, switch off the heat. The karah should fall from the spoon as a thick pudding.

9. Garnish with saffron or cardamom according to your personal preference, and serve immediately. Best enjoyed fresh and with good company!

*"Indu's secret to judging when
the semolina is cooked is when
you start to smell the aroma and
it fills the room."*

Imlee (tamarind) chutney

Indu uses this lip-smacking condiment to dress aloo papdi chaat (savoury yoghurt snack – see p179). Some of the other dadimas in this book also make imlee chutney and serve it with snacks like samosas and pakoras.

As highlighted in Indu's story, she was fortunate to learn her mother-in-law's culinary secrets, and imlee chutney is one of those treasured, passed-down recipes. Indu's mother-in-law, the quintessential matriarch and cook, lovingly prepares a large pot of this chutney to share with the family. Although you can now buy ready-made tamarind chutney, nothing beats the homemade version.

For this recipe, you'll need to use tamarind pulp. Enclosed in the brittle brown pods of the tamarind fruit, the pulp is known for its sticky texture and sweet and sour taste. It's sold as a block and available in good Indian supermarkets – buy the dry block and not the wet block. The secret to making this chutney is knowing the right balance between sweet and sour ingredients to mellow the pungency of the tamarind. I've spoken to some dadimas who quite like the tanginess of tamarind and others who lean towards a sweeter taste. I've given quantities below which achieve a sweet and sour taste, which I love. You'll need to taste the chutney once it's almost ready and adjust the spices to taste. I've added garam masala and cumin powder to Indu's mother-in-law's recipe, and used a little less ginger powder and sugar.

Consistency, again, varies to personal family tastes. However, for this recipe, the chutney should be a medium, rich consistency and a dark brown colour (when it cools, it thickens up, so don't make it too thick during cooking).

Store note: Imlee chutney keeps well in the fridge for a good month. Refrigerate in an airtight jar or screw-top bottle. Alternatively, freeze in an airtight container.

Prepare ahead: The tamarind block needs soaking ahead of time.

Makes around 250-270ml of tamarind chutney (medium consistency)
200g tamarind block
Boiling water, 1-1.2 litres

Flavouring – adjust to taste:
180g brown sugar
Half teaspoon salt
Pinch red chilli powder
Pinch ginger powder

Pinch garam masala
Quarter teaspoon cumin seeds, dry roasted until fragrant then ground to a powder

1. Place the tamarind block in a large, heavy-based saucepan (the same one you will be cooking in). Soak in around 550ml of boiling water (enough to just cover the tamarind block) for 4 hours at room temperature.
2. Now, cook the tamarind. Place the saucepan, as it is, over a medium heat and bring to a boil.
3. Simmer the block for 20 minutes until it looks like a squishy pulp and has softened. Stir occasionally to break up the block.
4. Stir in around 400-500ml of boiling water (never cold) so that the chutney is a medium consistency.
5. Stir in the sugar and spices over a low heat, then simmer for 10-12 minutes.
6. Strain the pulp through a large sieve into a mixing bowl. Stir it as you strain to help push the liquid out of the pulp. Add a little boiling water to any remaining thick pulp, and strain until satisfied that you've squeezed out as much as you can.
7. Discard the lumpy pulp left in the sieve. Return the liquid of the pulp to the saucepan.
8. Taste and add spices or sugar accordingly.
9. Simmer until the chutney has a glazed appearance, a medium consistency and coats the back of a spoon.
10. Allow to cool then transfer to a clean, airtight container and refrigerate. Use your homemade imlee chutney to garnish aloo papdi chaat or as a condiment with Indian fried snacks.

Aloo papdi chaat

Yes, it's quite a mouthful: 'aloo papdi chaat'. A direct translation just doesn't do it justice, so you can have fun with the street food name. This really is a refreshing treat, made with layers of flour crackers, potato cubes, chickpeas, yoghurt, tamarind sauce and other seasonings. The great news is that it's deceivingly easy to prepare, and presentation-wise, it has that 'wow' factor!

This is one of Indu's favourite starter dishes for parties. It's crucial that chaat is assembled and garnished just before serving, otherwise it will become soggy and lose its presentation. For this reason, it's one of the few dishes in this book which doesn't suit being prepared ahead or saving it as leftovers – just make as much as you need. Indu likes to serve her chaat on a flat serving plate so that the layers of ingredients are visible.

Do prepare the individual ingredients ahead of time. You can buy readymade papdi (flour crackers) from some Indian supermarkets, under the name 'chaat papdi'. I've provided you with the homemade recipe just in case you have difficulty acquiring them. I shouldn't really write this (so don't listen Indu), but if you want a real cheat which still tastes good, you can cut flour tortillas into small rectangles, and fry them until golden brown.

Serves 8

200g papdi (flour crackers) – usually sold under the name of 'chaat papdi' in Indian supermarkets. Alternatively, to make your own, see recipe overleaf)
1 medium-sized white potato (or potatoes equating to 250g), boiled, peeled and cut into half-inch cubes
120g cooked chickpeas
360-400g natural yoghurt, stirred in a bowl with salt to taste, until smooth

Quarter teaspoon red chilli powder (or to taste; alternatively, use paprika)
Half teaspoon black salt (usually sold under the name of kala namak or Himalayan black salt in Indian supermarkets)
150-170ml imlee (tamarind) chutney
Handful fresh coriander leaves, chopped, to garnish

Prepare ahead: *Do prepare the tamarind chutney, potatoes and flour crackers ahead of time.*

1. Place the papdi (flour crackers) on your serving dish as a thin first layer.
2. Place the potato chunks evenly across the papdi.
3. Spoon the chickpeas over the potatoes to complete the base of your chaat.
4. Now to dress the chaat. Spoon over the yoghurt in lines, leaving gaps in between.
5. Sprinkle the red chilli powder (or paprika) and black salt over the yoghurt.
6. Spoon the imlee chutney in the gaps between the yoghurt.
7. Garnish with fresh coriander.
8. Serve immediately and share with good company.

Recipe continued overleaf.

Aloo papdi chaat (continued)

To make the papdi (flour crackers):

For the dough: *See 'for the pastry' in Bholi's samosas recipe, p71-72. Omit the fenugreek from the ingredients and follow steps 1-3 to make the dough.*

Oil, for deep frying

Prepare your workstation: You need a clean, dry surface with plenty of room to roll the dough – ideally next to your cooker. Keep your flour for coating in a wide bowl. Line a plate with two pieces of kitchen roll for the fried papdi.

1. Heat the oil for deep frying whilst you roll out the dough.
2. Divide the dough into 3 pieces. Take one piece and roll into a ball shape using the palms of your hands. Lightly coat the ball in flour then flatten.
3. Roll out a small circle of around 3 inches in diameter then coat in flour again. Roll out a large, thin circle no thicker than 2mm (the size doesn't matter as it will be cut later). Use the same rolling technique as you would for a roti (chapatti) – use a fluid rolling motion with even pressure, then flip and roll on the other side.
4. Use a fork to generously prick the surface of the rolled out circle (this stops the papdi from puffing up when fried). Transfer the circle to a chopping board.
5. Use a large, sharp knife to cut the dough into small rectangles of around 4cm by 2cm.
6. Check that the oil is hot enough by dropping in a tiny ball of dough – it should rise to the top fairly quickly.
7. Drop each piece of papdi into the oil carefully. Deep fry over a moderate heat until light golden brown. Turn once.
8. Drain excess oil using a slotted spoon, remove and place on the plate lined with kitchen roll.
9. Repeat steps 3-8 to make the remaining papdi.
10. Leave to cool, and use as the base for your aloo papdi chaat, or as a cheeky snack with a mug of masala chai.

"This really is a refreshing treat, made with layers of flour crackers, potato cubes, chickpeas, yoghurt, tamarind sauce and other seasonings. It's deceivingly easy to prepare, and presentation-wise, it has that 'wow' factor!"

Paneer with peppers

Indu is really fussy about each and every dish she makes. Her recipe for paneer, a mild Indian cheese, is no different. Whilst Indu is a firm believer that a good tharka (masala base) is the foundation to every dish, she is keen to stress that she cooks each tharka slightly differently, so that her dishes have an individual flavouring. She's not one to batch-make or freeze a generic tharka mixture, as she still cooks fresh on the day. For paneer, Indu prefers to use only ginger, not garlic.

When Indu used to entertain a lot, paneer was a must on her menu, served with a daal, rotis, rice, yoghurt, salad and spring lamb (see Indu's spring lamb recipe on p185). Indu always manages to cook her paneer so that it's soft but with the pieces sitting firmly. Her secret is to cover the paneer whilst cooking so that it softens slowly. She also advises switching off the heat as soon as the paneer softens, so that the pieces maintain their shape.

People take pride in their different styles of cooking paneer, and it varies between regions in India — some versions are quite runny, others are intended to be dry, like paneer tikka. Paneer is versatile in complementing other ingredients like saag (see Kamla's recipe on p205) to make delicious saag paneer, or with peas to make mattar paneer. You can even make paneer pakoras and samosas. Indu's paneer has a dry-style tharka (masala base) which serves as a coating and glaze. Indu does not like to overdo it with the tomatoes so that the paneer is the hero of the dish.

Although I haven't included the recipe in this book, you can make fresh paneer at home using milk. Indu now buys fresh paneer from the supermarkets. It's so easy to prepare — simply chop the paneer block into cubes, or buy the pre-cubed bag.

Indu likes to cook the paneer on its own. I've tweaked the recipe by adding slightly more tomatoes than Indu, and by including a few vegetables. I like the vibrancy of red peppers as they remind me of summer barbecues. You can also add peas, sweetcorn, or mixed vegetables.

Freeze note: Paneer freezes well.

Serves 4 as a main course, or 6-7 as part of other dishes
4-5 tablespoons rapeseed oil
1 teaspoon cumin seeds
1 white onion, sliced thickly
3 green finger chillies, topped and snapped in half
25g fresh ginger, peeled and blended

1 teaspoon salt (or to taste)
1 heaped teaspoon turmeric powder (haldi)
1 level teaspoon paprika
Quarter teaspoon red chilli powder (or to taste)
1 teaspoon garam masala
100g plum tomatoes, blended

1 red pepper, sliced into 2-inch rectangular chunks
50g frozen peas and sweetcorn (optional)
500g paneer, chopped into cubes of around 1 inch
Handful fresh coriander, chopped, to garnish

1. Heat the oil, then add the cumin seeds. Allow them to sizzle before stirring in the onions.
2. Cover and cook the onions on a low heat until they start to soften. Stir once to check that nothing is sticking.
3. Add the green chillies and ginger. Cook until the onions are medium brown.
4. Add a splash of water before adding the spices — only add half of the garam masala. Cook for 1 minute.
5. Stir through the tomatoes and cook over a medium heat until the tharka is ready. This is when the consistency thickens and oil bubbles form around the mixture. Then add peppers/mixed vegetables (if using) and cook until softened.
6. Stir in the paneer chunks, coating them with tharka.
7. Cover and simmer for around 10-12 minutes. Stir once or twice to ensure nothing is sticking. As soon as the paneer chunks soften, switch off the heat and stir through the remaining garam masala.
8. Garnish with fresh coriander and serve hot.

Mushroom subji

Indu loves mushroom subji as a flavoursome sidekick to her main dishes. She usually serves it alongside daal, spring lamb, rotis (chapattis), a salad and yoghurt, as part of a full meal. It's important that the mushrooms are kept fairly chunky (quartered) so that they can withstand cooking and not become soggy. Indu never adds water as the mushrooms release their own. She prefers to make this dish in a tall, medium-sized saucepan with a lid.

Serves 4

3 cloves garlic

25g ginger, peeled

2 green finger chillies (or to taste)

4-5 tablespoons rapeseed oil

1 level teaspoon cumin seeds

1 small white onion, roughly sliced

120g tinned plum tomatoes, blended

Three quarter teaspoon salt (or to taste)

1 teaspoon turmeric powder (haldi)

Three quarter teaspoon paprika

Half teaspoon ground black pepper

1 teaspoon garam masala

300g closed cup white mushrooms

Handful fresh coriander, to garnish

1. Blitz the garlic, ginger and green chillies in a small blender and set aside.
2. Heat the oil in a saucepan and add the cumin seeds. Allow them to sizzle then stir in the onions.
3. Cover and simmer for 4-5 minutes until the onions start to soften.
4. Stir in the garlic, ginger and green chillies. Cover and cook for 2 minutes on a low heat.
5. Add the tomatoes and cook over a moderate heat for 2 minutes.
6. Add the salt, haldi, paprika, pepper and half a teaspoon of the garam masala. Cook over a medium heat, until the tharka (onion masala base) thickens and oil bubbles form around the mixture.
7. Stir in the mushrooms and ensure they are fully coated with tharka.
8. Cover and simmer on a very low heat for 10 minutes. Stir halfway through.
9. Stir over a medium-high heat to cook off excess water. The mushrooms should be glazed with tharka.
10. Stir through the remaining garam masala, garnish with the coriander and serve hot.

Spring lamb

Indu takes immense pride in cooking her spring lamb dish, and believes there is a real art to making it well. Marrying into a family who were big on meat, young Indu very quickly perfected her meat dishes with the guidance of her talented mother-in-law. Indu's winning combination suggestion is spring lamb, served with yellow daal, aloo bhengan (see recipe on p48), yoghurt, a salad and rotis (chapattis).

For this dish, Indu always opts for chunks of spring lamb shoulder with chops. She believes that the chops add depth in texture, appearance and flavour. When I learnt this dish from Indu, she was not at all impressed that the butcher had forgotten to add the lamb chops to the bag. We couldn't continue the cooking until she had the chops! However, she stresses that you can leave them out altogether if you prefer, or if you're catering for kids who don't like meat on the bone.

Indu advises to stick with one cut and type of meat as cooking times may differ. The texture to this dish needs to be fairly dry, so don't overdo it when it comes to adding water. The lamb should be succulent and glazed with tharka. To save time and effort, ask your butcher to chop the spring lamb shoulder into chunks.

Use a stainless steel karahi. If not, use a bowl-shaped, heavy-based pan with a lid.

Freeze note: This dish freezes well. For best results, re-heat in a saucepan and a little boiling water.

Serves 6-8
5 tablespoons rapeseed oil
1 teaspoon cumin seeds
2 medium-sized white onions, finely chopped
6 garlic cloves
40g fresh ginger, peeled
4 green finger chillies, topped and snapped in half (or to taste)
Handful fresh fenugreek leaves

(methi), finely chopped (or 1 and a half tablespoons dried fenugreek – sold as kasuri methi in Indian supermarkets)
1 teaspoon salt (or to taste)
1 heaped teaspoon turmeric powder (haldi)
Half teaspoon coriander powder
Half teaspoon paprika
1 heaped teaspoon garam masala

250g plum tomatoes, blended
Squirt of tomato purée
500g spring lamb shoulder chops
500g spring lamb shoulder, cut into chunks
Half cup to 1 cup of boiling water
Handful fresh coriander, plus extra for garnish

1. Blitz the garlic and ginger in a small blender and set aside.
2. Heat the oil in your karahi/pan, then add the cumin seeds and wait for them to sizzle.
3. Stir in the onions, cover and cook on a low heat until soft and medium brown. The secret to this tharka is to 'bhun' (brown) and soften the onions for longer than we usually would for a vegetable dish. Stir occasionally to ensure nothing is sticking and add a splash of water if required.
4. Stir in the garlic, ginger and green chillies, cover and cook for 1-2 minutes on a low heat.
5. Add the fenugreek and spices, but just add half a teaspoon of the garam masala. Cook for 1 minute.
6. Stir in the tomatoes and tomato purée. Cover and cook on a low heat until the tharka is ready. This is when the consistency thickens and small oil bubbles form around the mixture. Stir occasionally to ensure nothing is sticking.
7. Stir in the lamb over a medium heat, coating it fully with the tharka. Use a wide folding motion to stir your lamb inwards. Indu says that stirring at this stage is crucial to getting good flavour into the lamb and getting rid of that 'meaty smell' before simmering!
8. Add enough boiling water to half-cover the lamb. You may need more or less depending on the pan you use – I add between three-quarters to one cup in a karahi. Add a small handful of the coriander and stir. Simmer for 1 hour, covered. Stir the lamb occasionally during this time and ensure there is always enough water in the pan. Add a little more boiling water if required – not too much as the end dish should have a fairly dry texture.
9. Test that the lamb is cooked through – it should be tender.
10. Stir constantly over a medium heat until excess liquid is cooked off and the meat is glazed with tharka. Stir in the remainder of the garam masala, garnish with coriander and serve hot.

Kamla

aloo gobi
cholay
kamla's classic kadhi
indian stuffed peppers
saag
kamla's soft fluffy rotis

amla was born in 1948 in the Punjab, India. Alongside my dadima, she has been a key inspiration to me with her incredible strength of character (and dry sense of humour to go with it). And so, last but not least, I conclude this book with my dearest nanima (maternal grandmother).

Those who are closest to Kamla would describe her as resilient, direct in speech, and highly independent (with OCD for cleanliness!). At the same time, she's laid-back and open-minded – a really 'cool nan'! She loves fashion and is fussy on quality – her favourite accessory is her Harrods shopping bag.

Kamla lives alone in the Midlands – sadly she lost her husband (my nanaji, Jagdish) at the young age of 52 to alcoholism. Most of Kamla's family do not live locally, but Kamla is adamant on staying put where she has built her life. She is a proud mother to three highly-educated and successful children, and five grandchildren. She has been a self-made businesswoman for 25 years, running a fabric and haberdashery business. I have fond memories of visiting my nanima's shop as a young girl – except when I made mistakes on her cash till, of course! Kamla's mental maths skills are still faster than the calculator at times! Kamla is a creature of routine, and after a hard day at work, she unwinds with Indian TV dramas and games on her tablet.

Another part of Kamla's daily routine is organising her complex medication combination. Apart from being a heart patient, she lives with a constant nerve pain in her mouth, which results in sleepless nights and low energy levels. Because of this, Kamla no longer takes pleasure in eating the foods that she once used to enjoy. Nonetheless, if Kamla knows that her family are visiting, she goes into superwoman action mode, rolls up her sleeves, and creates a mouth-watering feast with their favourite dishes. She cooks at the crack of dawn, before she catches the bus to work. When I visited on her recent birthday (ready to treat her), she had rustled up my traditional Indian favourites, and laid them out in pots before my arrival.

Kamla talks with admiration and respect about her father, who was a strict but loving military man, holding a senior position. Living in an extended family, as sibling number four of six, she was quite sheltered from early responsibilities, though she recalls the years of hardship. The family were left bankrupt when Kamla's father, after retiring, entered a business deal with a 'friend'. Being a highly principled man of his word, Kamla's father worked long hours, but was betrayed. Kamla reflects with sadness on memories of her devastated father, having to sell off her mother's jewellery in order to support the family.

For Kamla, her life in India was a simple one. She was a quiet, observant girl who enjoyed studying. "At school, no make-up or nail polish was allowed, and we didn't wear fancy clothes. These days it's all about the 'rat race' and making more money!" (translated).

In 1968, aged 20, Kamla entered the married chapter of her life in the UK. After an arranged marriage to Jagdish, she moved from India to the Midlands, and lived with her extended family. Settling in was hard, not least because of the unfamiliar surroundings and people, cold weather and living in a home with no hot water or a bath. To make matters worse, only a week after her move, Kamla was grieving at the sad news of her father's death.

Living with her husband and brother-in-law, Kamla would wash their clothes by hand as they did not have a washing machine. The toilet was outside of the house, and they used public baths to have a shower. She didn't have friends – her sister-in-law became her closest confidante.

Kamla was overjoyed about moving house, as her second home had central heating, a bath and an indoor toilet. Tensions arose, however, from the work involved in building a new home which needed a lot of attention.

Kamla and Jagdish both worked hard to make ends meet. Kamla found work at a sewing factory doing 'piece work', which she hated. She worked there for four months until her first daughter was born. Kamla then found work as a packer in the well-known John Players cigarette factory in Nottingham. For her 40-hour week, Kamla earned three pounds and four shillings. After giving birth to her second daughter and youngest son, Kamla returned to work in the factory for a further 17 years, until she took voluntary redundancy and established her own business. Her stubborn, independent, and hard-working personality traits were totally suited to her being her own boss. In her subtly dynamic style, she would liaise with suppliers, attend meetings, and organise finances – all whilst keeping up with the latest fabric trends and running a slick family operation at home.

Jagdish adored Kamla's home-cooked Indian food and insisted on fresh meals every day. It's safe to say that I could have written a book on just Kamla's recipes. From her delicious lamb chops, to tasty aloo gobi (potato and cauliflower), bhindi (okra) and pakoras (bhajis), food was high on Jagdish's daily agenda. After a day at the Royal Ordnance Factory as an engineer, he lived for the dining experience, where variety, quality ingredients and taste were the three magic components. Jagdish, a humble man, would always sit cross-legged to eat his dinner on the floor. He had a particular pickiness about food combinations: a dry subji (vegetable dish) had to be accompanied with something liquid (such as lentils or kidney beans), while meat dishes were to be accompanied with something dry, and yoghurt and salad were a must. His fussiness extended to eating each dish in separate bowls, and chapattis being served hot, straight off the tawa (hot plate).

After his Friday night trips to the local pub, it was not uncommon for Jagdish to come home and ask Kamla to rustle up some of her fabulous food for him and his friends. Kamla always obliged and cooked whatever he asked for in her hospitable style. She says: "He would make such a mess of the kitchen when he cooked that it would save me time in the morning if I just did it myself!" Kamla remembers the times that Jagdish sweetly thought he'd save her cooking, but would leave grease marks on the cooker from making curried beans, bacon and eggs after a night out.

Jagdish's death in 1999 took a huge toll on Kamla's lifestyle, and triggered her decline in health. Despite battling grief and poor health, all in a very private manner, proud Kamla refused to give up her business and move closer to her children. In Indian culture, being a widow can bring with it some unfortunate social customs, one of them being to dress very plainly. Only recently has my nanima, after years of persistence from her children and grandchildren, started to introduce a few colours into her wardrobe. With her three children now married and settled, Kamla lives independently. She is fortunate to have lived opposite neighbours, who have become her family – she trusts, loves and respects them deeply.

Kamla has changed her style of cooking to suit her dietary needs as a single vegetarian, and more health-conscious person. With the onset of her mouth pain, she has cut back on chillies, and now opts for plainer foods.

Kamla doesn't mince her words when it comes to giving opinions on food, as her standards are so high and her culinary experience, extensive. She'd be the toughest food critic on MasterChef! This honesty extends to all areas of her life, and she is the only one in the family who can get away with telling someone that they've put on a few pounds and should be exercising more!

My nanima is a wise, straight-talking woman who has experienced hardship and pain. What's most important to her in life? Her independence. "I've been independent for many years," she says, "I've worked hard to look after my kids and myself my whole life."

Kamla's advice to her grandchildren is to respect one's elders, and learn from their mistakes. As chilled out and easy-going as she is, she still says: "If you don't listen, you'll just have to learn the hard way!" She also advises all young people to learn the art of cooking, as too much restaurant food can be costly and unhealthy.

Kamla's final piece of advice is rooted in personal experiences – "You must develop the wisdom and courage to know when to ignore someone's negative words and actions, and know when to invest energy in battling it out". To clarify her meaning, she draws on a well-cited Punjabi analogy: *lassi aur larai da ke vadanai* – exacerbating an argument just leads to further disagreement, so don't argue with people when they are in a state of anger.

With Kamla's fussy culinary standards in mind, I leave you to have fun with some classic dishes in her chapter.

Aloo gobi
(Potatoes & cauliflower)

Kamla's husband, Jagdish, loved her aloo gobi. He used to say there is a real art to making it, and his criteria included: well-flavoured potatoes and cauliflower, a good helping of ginger, soft, but not soggy or mashed, cauliflower florets and potatoes.

Jagdish always preferred a smaller ratio of potatoes to cauliflower, which is why Kamla still cooks it with fewer potatoes. She used to cook this dish a lot for Jagdish and her brother-in-law, and cauliflower was a staple weekly vegetable in her fridge.

Kamla's key advice to making this dish, is never to add tomatoes or water, as this makes the aloo gobi soggy. Her secret is to simmer the dish over a low heat, and not to over-stir. She used to serve it for Jagdish with daal and fresh rotis. She does not recommend freezing it, and says it tastes best fresh, or the day after. For best results, Kamla recommends using a shallow, wide frying pan with a lid.

Serves 4
300g medium-sized white potatoes (new potatoes or any suitable for boiling)
1 medium-sized cauliflower (just over 400g)
5 tablespoons rapeseed oil
1 large onion, diced

2 cloves garlic, crushed
35g fresh ginger, peeled and grated
2 green finger chillies, finely chopped (or to taste)
1 heaped teaspoon cumin seeds
1 and a half teaspoons salt (or to taste)
2 teaspoons haldi (turmeric powder)
1 and a quarter teaspoons garam

masala
Handful of chopped coriander, to garnish

Prepare ahead: *To save time, cut and wash the cauliflower a few hours in advance of cooking. This way, it has plenty of time to dry.*

1. Peel the potatoes, chop into small chunks and set aside. Cut the cauliflower into medium-sized florets, wash, and leave to dry on a plate lined with kitchen roll. Kamla does this so that the florets are dry before going into the pan.

2. Make a start on your tharka (onion masala base). Heat the oil in a wide, non-stick pan, and add the onions once hot. Stir regularly over a moderate heat until light brown.

3. Add the garlic, ginger and green chillies. Cook until the onions are medium brown. Kamla always adds less garlic than ginger for aloo gobi, and sometimes omits garlic altogether.

4. Stir through the cumin seeds, 1 teaspoon of the salt and 1 teaspoon of the haldi, fully coating the onions. Cook the spices for 2 minutes, stirring regularly.

5. Stir in the potatoes over a moderate heat, ensuring each one is coated with spices. Potatoes go first as they take longer to cook than the cauliflower.

6. Stir through the remaining salt and haldi, ensuring the potatoes are coated with colour.

7. Cover and simmer for 15 minutes, or until the potatoes are half-cooked. Check and stir in between to ensure that nothing is sticking.

8. Carefully stir in the cauliflower florets, coating them fully with the spices. (Make sure that the cauliflower is dry before adding – pat dry with a kitchen roll).

9. Cover and simmer for 10 minutes, or until the potatoes and cauliflower are almost cooked. Stir half way during this time.

10. Stir through the garam masala. Cover and simmer for 7-10 minutes until the vegetables are soft enough to pierce with a knife and fully cooked.

11. Garnish with coriander and serve immediately.

Cholay
(Chickpeas)

Making cholay is a cooking process that Kamla takes great pride in. Kamla prefers to cook chickpeas from their raw state, rather than using the tinned variety. Her late husband, a real Punjabi food connoisseur, only ate fresh chickpeas, as he could apparently taste the difference! I won't tell Kamla I wrote this, but if you really don't have the time to make fresh chickpeas, simply follow the recipe for the tharka (masala onion base), add your tinned chickpeas and simmer until ready.

Kamla has several secrets to making the perfect cholay. She soaks the raw chickpeas overnight in loose water, with either half a teaspoon of bicarbonate soda (for the quantity below) or one teaspoon of salt. Kamla also adds three teabags to the water – this is her top tip for introducing that rich colour to the dish. Once soaked, Kamla slow-cooks the chickpeas from morning till evening whilst she's at work (judge this by the power of your slow cooker until they are soft). She prefers to cook her tharka separately, rather than adding all of the ingredients to the slow-cooker. It's a little more time, but she likes to have control over the consistency of her tharka and ensure each ingredient is cooked to the stage she likes it.

I prefer to use the pressure cooker for this recipe as it saves time. However, if you prefer the convenience of slow-cooking, I have given both options in the recipe below.

Cholay is a superstar main dish in itself, served with rice or roti, along with a good helping of yoghurt. As a starter it's also the perfect accompaniment to aloo tikkis and samosas (see Bholi's recipes p68 and p71).

Serves 5-6
400g raw chickpeas
Approximately 1 litre cold water
3 English breakfast teabags
1 teaspoon salt, or half teaspoon
bicarbonate soda
4 medium-sized cloves garlic, whole

For the tharka:
4 tablespoons rapeseed oil
1 heaped teaspoon cumin seeds
1 onion, chopped
30g ginger, peeled and grated
1 level teaspoon pomegranate
powder (optional)

Half teaspoon paprika
1 teaspoon salt (or to taste)
Half teaspoon ground black pepper
400g tinned plum tomatoes, blended
1 teaspoon garam masala
Fresh coriander, to garnish

1. Soak the chickpeas overnight as follows: add the chickpeas, water, teabags and salt (or bicarbonate soda) to the pot of your slow cooker or pressure cooker. Stir once so that the teabags release their colour, cover and leave to soak.

2. Now for cooking the raw chickpeas. Remove the teabags and discard, then add the garlic cloves to the chickpeas. Pressure cook, observing the relevant safety measures, until the chickpeas are soft. They should give quite easily if you pinch them. You may need to check after the first pressure cook, and cook for another few whistles. If slow-cooking, set to a high heat and cook until soft, as above. Kamla's slow cooker is quite powerful and cooks the chickpeas in about 9-10 hours.

3. Once the chickpeas have cooked, switch them off whilst you make the tharka in a separate saucepan.

4. Heat the oil in a saucepan and once hot, add the cumin seeds and allow to sizzle, before adding the onions.

5. Cook the onions over a moderate heat until light brown, stirring regularly.

6. Stir in the ginger and cook for 2 minutes, or until the ginger has browned slightly.

7. Stir through the pomegranate powder, paprika, salt and pepper, ensuring the onions are fully coated in the spices. Cook for 2 minutes, stirring regularly.

8. Stir through the tomatoes over a medium-high heat and cook until the tharka is a medium consistency. You'll know the tharka is ready when oil bubbles are visible around the mixture, where they have separated from the tomatoes. When you stir, it should feel as if the tharka has come together.

9. Pour the tharka into the cooked chickpeas and stir through – you'll see the colour change.

10. Now, it's time to simmer the chickpeas and tharka together. If slow cooking, cook on a low setting for a further 30 minutes so that the flavours are infused. If you used the pressure cooker, then simmer uncovered (as though it's a standard pan) for 20 minutes. You may wish to transfer the chickpeas to a separate pan depending on the size of your pressure cooker.

11. Taste for salt, then add the garam masala and stir through, before switching off your cooking appliance.

12. At this stage, Kamla has a secret tip to thicken the tharka and create a rich consistency: remove your cooking pot/pressure cooker from the heat. Then use a hand-blender inside the pot to briefly blend some of the chickpeas so that no more than a handful are mashed. Push the hand-blender right into the sauce so that it doesn't splatter everywhere!

13. Serve hot and garnish with fresh coriander.

Freeze note: Cholay is a great dish to freeze. Thaw and re-heat in a saucepan.

"Cholay is a superstar main dish in itself, served with rice or roti, along with a good helping of yoghurt. As a starter it's also the perfect accompaniment to aloo tikkis and samosas."

Kamla's classic kadhi

Kadhi (pronounced 'curry') is a classic, timeless dish which is made from a gram flour and yoghurt-based sauce, to which pakoras (bhajis) are added. I always ask Kamla, my nanima (grandmother), to make me some when I visit her. Saag and kadhi are two of her traditional specialities, and she always cooks both dishes in large quantities, as my late nanaji (grandfather) would insist on sharing them with local friends or relatives – he took great pride in showing off her culinary skills. Even today, Kamla still makes a generous quantity of kadhi, and shares it out, remembering my nanaji's generous hospitality with food.

Kamla's kadhi has two key cooking parts: the pakoras and the yoghurt sauce. As Kamla works full-time, she usually makes the pakoras on one day, and then the sauce the following. It's important that the yoghurt for the sauce is slightly sour, as this is the secret to the sauce's distinctive taste. To achieve this, Kamla leaves her yoghurt out the night before cooking. For the pakoras, I direct you to Santosh's 'aloo palak pakoras' recipe (p50). Having learnt how to make them from both of my grandmothers, I can safely say that the pakoras are equally delicious. If you already have some pakoras frozen from Santosh's recipe, use them.

For ayurvedic reasons, Kamla adds fenugreek seeds, a pinch of asafoetida, and more garlic and ginger than she usually would, as she says it aids digestion. Kamla says that the sauce of the kadhi should be showcased, as therein lies the beauty. Therefore, it's best not to add too many pakoras to the sauce. With each serving of a pakora, there should be a generous helping of sauce.

When Kamla cooks and talks about kadhi, I can't help but smile to myself at the pride she takes in this dish, but also how she appreciates its regional variations in India. For example, some people add sugar to their kadhi, but Kamla says that where she was raised in the Punjab, kadhi is known for its unique 'katta' (slightly sour) taste, so she would never do that! In short, this is a dish very close to her heart, and one which connects her with her northern Indian heritage.

Kamla likes plain boiled rice as an accompaniment to kadhi. She insists that you use a large, stock pot-style pan to boil the kadhi, as it needs plenty of space to bubble and simmer. When I learnt this recipe, I saw a lot of multitasking going on, which of course is no problem for Kamla, who has been making kadhi for many years. From the length of the recipe, it may not look like it, but I have simplified Kamla's steps a little! I've made tiny tweaks to Kamla's recipe by adding mustard seeds, curry leaves and tomatoes – something which I've learnt from other talented dadimas. With elegant confidence, Kamla says that kadhi is a really rewarding dish to make, but there is an art to it. She emphasises that it requires love, patience, and attention to detail. With these words of wisdom, I leave you now to recreate this winter warmer in your own kitchen.

See the classic kadhi recipe overleaf.

Serves 8-10 as a main dish

Prepare ahead: *I strongly recommend preparing the pakoras a day in advance to save time and effort. Alternatively, make and freeze the pakoras, then thaw and use as per method. The yoghurt for the kadhi sauce will need to be left out overnight ideally, unless it's already sour-tasting yoghurt.*

Pakoras:
See Santosh's recipe for aloo palak pakoras (with the quantity specified, you will only need around half of the pakoras, but I always make a batch and freeze them). (See p50)

Kadhi sauce:
1kg natural yoghurt (ideally the runny yoghurt, not the set one)
1 tablespoon fresh lemon juice, plus extra to taste
100g gram flour (known as 'besan' in Indian supermarkets)
Half cup of cold water
5 tablespoons rapeseed oil
1 heaped teaspoon cumin seeds
1 teaspoon mustard seeds
1 teaspoon fenugreek seeds
Pinch of asafoetida/hing (a pinch – no more!)
1 large onion, diced into medium-sized chunks
5 cloves garlic, finely chopped
35g fresh ginger, peeled and grated

2 green finger chillies, finely chopped (or to taste)
1 teaspoon salt (or to taste)
1 teaspoon pomegranate powder (anardana)
2 tablespoons turmeric powder (haldi)
5 curry leaves (optional)
100g plum tomatoes, blended
1-1.5 litres boiling water
1 teaspoon garam masala
Coriander, to garnish

1. The night before cooking: mix the yoghurt in a large, deep mixing bowl until it reaches a smooth consistency. Add the lemon juice, cover, and leave out overnight at room temperature (don't leave for more than 24 hours).

2. When you're ready to start cooking, prepare the yoghurt mixture for the sauce. Sift the gram flour over your bowl of yoghurt (the more gram flour you add, the thicker the sauce will be and the more water required later). Add half a cup of cold water to loosen the consistency. Use a hand-blender to blend the mixture until it reaches a smooth consistency with no lumps. This can get messy, so do it over the sink if possible. Set aside whilst you make the tharka (onion masala base).

3. Heat the oil in a large, deep pot. Add the cumin seeds and mustard seeds, allowing them to sizzle before adding the fenugreek seeds and asafoetida. Cook for 1 minute, stirring regularly.

4. Add the onions and cook until medium brown and softened, stirring regularly. Then stir in the garlic and ginger, cooking for 2 minutes with the onions.

5. Add the green chillies, salt, pomegranate powder, 1 tablespoon of the turmeric powder and the curry leaves. Stir regularly over a low heat for 2 minutes, before adding the tomatoes to complete your tharka.

6. Stir regularly until the tharka is ready. This is when the oil separates from the tomatoes in bubbles around the mixture, and the tharka has thickened.

7. Boil your kettle now with 1.5 litres of water.

8. Carefully tip the yoghurt mixture into the pan. Cook for 2-3 minutes, stirring constantly.

For the next steps, we'll be adding boiling water gradually. You will need just over a litre as a base, and the remaining half a litre is a cushion in case the sauce becomes a little thick (it will also make a larger quantity). It's important that you don't leave your cooker unattended until the simmering stage, as the kadhi sauce can easily boil over. Kamla advises that boiling water is really important – if there's not enough, the sauce can taste of uncooked gram flour.

9. Add around 500ml of the hot water, stirring over a moderate heat until you feel the sauce thicken up slightly. Watch out for the spitting action from the pan.

10. Add the remaining turmeric powder at this stage. We're aiming for a colour like Dijon mustard. Add a further 500ml of hot water, stirring until the sauce starts bubbling around the edges and thickening further.

11. Bring to a boil (this is the part to stand by your cooker; it won't take long as the water is already boiling). When it comes to a boil, reduce the heat to medium and stir until the bubbles at the surface have reduced.

12. Simmer on a very low heat, partially covered, for 15 minutes.

13. Taste the kadhi. It should have a delicate but noticeable sour taste. If you prefer more of a sour taste, add a tablespoon of fresh lemon juice.

14. Simmer for 1 hour, partially covered, until the sauce is of a medium consistency. Stir occasionally in between to check that there is no sticking. If the sauce is on the thick side and is sticking, use the remaining boiling water to loosen the consistency.

15. Simmer for a further hour, until the sauce has a rich, medium consistency. Stir occasionally. The longer you can leave it to simmer, the better it will taste.

16. Stir in the pakoras – add enough so that they are fully coated and swimming in the sauce. Add the garam masala and stir through.

17. Serve immediately and garnish with coriander. Good luck trying to resist seconds!

Freeze note: Kamla doesn't recommend freezing kadhi, but it lasts in the fridge for a couple of days.

"When Kamla cooks and talks about kadhi, I can't help but smile to myself at the pride she takes in this dish. This is a dish very close to her heart, and one which connects her with her northern Indian heritage."

Indian stuffed peppers

Making stuffed peppers reminds Kamla of the days when she hosted her dinner parties. They are always a hit as they look attractive, are healthy and flavoursome.

Kamla emphasises that you can add pretty much any filling of your choice. The secret is that the filling should have a moist, but still fairly dry consistency. The two fillings I have given in this recipe are Kamla favourites: one being meat-free mince and peas, the other being potato and peas. Kamla is vegetarian, but used to make keema stuffed peppers when her children lived with her – see Angela's keema recipe (p103) if you want to try this variation. If you ever have left over filling mixture, use it in a paratha (see Sheila's recipe on p143).

Kamla is particular when it comes to sealing the peppers – she likes the top (or 'lid') of the pepper to be pushed down like a button, so that it's compact during cooking. She lightly glazes the peppers so that they can soften, and have a slightly chargrilled effect on the skin once cooked.

I find stuffed peppers so versatile for casual dining, or a sit-down meal. They go down a treat with other casual party dishes, like Arun's corn on the cob and Bholi's aloo tikkis or samosas.

Prepare ahead: If you're pressed for time, prepare the filling a day in advance and store it in the fridge. As a finished dish, stuffed peppers don't freeze well.

Makes 4 stuffed peppers
4 peppers (any colour you like;
I prefer 2 green and 2 red)
Rapeseed oil (for greasing the
outside of the peppers)

Meat-free mince filling:
4 tablespoons rapeseed oil
1 small onion, finely chopped
20g ginger, peeled and grated
1 teaspoon turmeric powder (haldi)
Half teaspoon red chilli powder (or
to taste)

Half teaspoon paprika
Half teaspoon salt (or to taste)
Half teaspoon ground black pepper
150g tinned plum tomatoes, blended
200g frozen meat-free mince
1 teaspoon dark soy sauce
100g frozen peas

1. Heat the oil, and then stir in the onions. Cook and stir regularly until light brown.
2. Add the ginger and cook for 2 minutes, stirring regularly.
3. Stir in the turmeric powder, red chilli powder, paprika, salt and pepper, coating the onions fully. Stir over a low heat for 2 minutes.
4. Add the tomatoes and cook over a moderate-high heat for 5 minutes until the tharka (onion masala base) thickens.
5. Add the meat-free mince, coat with the tharka and use your spoon to break up the mince in the pan.
6. Cook over a moderate heat for 10 minutes, stirring regularly to ensure the pieces have broken up completely and all are coated in the tharka. Then add the soy sauce.
7. Add the frozen peas and cook for a further 5 minutes.
8. Stir over a moderate-high heat until no excess water is visible around the pan and you have a medium-thick consistency.

Recipe continued overleaf.

Indian stuffed peppers (continued)

Potato filling:
4 tablespoons rapeseed oil
1 small onion, finely chopped
3 medium-sized garlic cloves, crushed
1 teaspoon salt (or to taste)
1 teaspoon pepper

1 level teaspoon pomegranate
powder (or mango powder)
1 tablespoon tomato purée
100g frozen peas
2 medium-sized white potatoes,
boiled, peeled and roughly mashed

1. Heat the oil, and then stir in the onions, cooking until light brown.
2. Add the garlic and cook for 1 minute, stirring regularly.
3. Stir in the salt, pepper and pomegranate powder, coating the onions fully. Cook for 1-2 minutes.
4. Add the tomato purée and stir through until it loosens up and coats the onions fully.
5. Add the frozen peas and stir through so they are glazed with the sauce.
6. Cook the peas for 5 minutes until soft, then add the potatoes.
7. Stir through, coating the potatoes with the spices.

Stuffing the peppers:
1. Cut the 'lids' for each pepper: Hold the pepper upright. Use a sharp knife to carefully cut a circle around the stem – don't be tempted to just slice the top off the pepper – it needs to be a tight-fitting lid. Place each lid next to its partner pepper. Discard the seeds.
2. Fill each pepper: spoon in your chosen filling. When half full, gently push down on the mixture with the back of your spoon to maximise space. Fill to the top, leaving enough space for the lid.
3. Place the correct lids onto each pepper, pushing down firmly into the grooves so that there are no gaps.
4. Rub some rapeseed oil onto the skins of the peppers so that they have a good glaze all over.
5. Place the peppers on an oven tray, sitting as upright as possible. Oven cook for 30 minutes at 180°C. Check halfway through and turn the peppers around – you should see the skin have a chargrilled, shrivelled effect as it softens. If you prefer firmer textured peppers, cook for just 20 minutes.
6. Serve hot, sliced in half or whole.

"Making stuffed peppers reminds Kamla of the days when she hosted her dinner parties. They are always a hit as they look attractive, are healthy and flavoursome."

Saag
(Cooked leafy vegetables)

I cannot hide the fact that Kamla's saag is my all-time favourite dish, along with her kadhi. With classic Punjabi dishes such as this, there's nowhere to hide if something goes wrong, but fortunately, Kamla has years of knowledge and experience to share. The word saag is sometimes used interchangeably with spinach in British Indian dining. But as Kamla says, traditional Punjabi saag actually refers to a mixture of cooked leafy green vegetables, including but not limited to spinach. Other possible ingredients may include mustard greens, kale, fenugreek, broccoli, brussels sprouts and spring greens. Cooked spinach by itself is best described as 'palak' (as in palak paneer). Kamla varies the ingredients she uses to make her saag, depending on seasonality and availability in shops. She likes to use the following combinations: mustard greens and spinach; broccoli and spinach; and kale and broccoli.

Kamla's favourite saag, however, is the traditional 'sarson ka saag'', which is made from mustard greens and spinach. This is the recipe I've given below. Mustard greens (sold under the name 'sarson' in Indian supermarkets) have a distinctive peppery taste. They are thicker, and take much longer to cook than spinach. This is why the traditional sarson ka saag requires a patient cook to do it real justice.

When the saag is at its simmering stage, Kamla watches snippets of her soap operas, popping back into the kitchen regularly to give it a stir. Patience in shopping is also needed when acquiring the mustard greens, as they sell out quickly where she lives. She sometimes visits two or three shops after a long day at work on a mustard greens hunt! Whenever I visit, Kamla always tells me the story of shopping for the greens, explaining how long it takes to buy and cook.

Mustard greens are most readily available in late winter/early spring when they're at their peak season. Kamla's secret is to simmer for a couple of hours. She likes a medium thick consistency – saag is meant to have this consistency. Although the texture will be thick when served, there needs to be enough water to cook the vegetables into a pulp-like texture, and to stop the saag sticking to the bottom of the pan. Kamla purées her greens using a potato masher and hand-blender – the potato masher works well for broccoli. She also likes to add a small handful of fresh fenugreek leaves (methi).

Although I've not shared the recipe for this bread, saag is traditionally served with makki di roti (cornmeal chapattis). However, it tastes just as delicious with Kamla's fluffy rotis. If you have leftover saag, you can vary the dish by adding chunks of paneer, chicken or boneless lamb. Cook this in the same saucepan as your tharka, then add the cooked saag. Make sure you use a large, deep cooking pan for the saag, as boiling water will be added in stages. Although this is a time-consuming recipe, saag is the perfect dish to be frozen, so I've suggested quantities for a large batch.

Note: Kamla batch prepares her saag and freezes it without the tharka (onion masala base). So that it has that fresh taste from frozen, Kamla makes the tharka just before serving, and then adds her saag to it.

See the saag recipe overleaf.

Saag (continued)

Makes 15-20 servings

You will need: *a hand-blender*

To make the saag:
3 bunches mustard greens (sold as
fresh bunches under the name of
'sarson' in Indian supermarkets),
washed, left to dry in a colander, and
chopped, stalks included
500g spinach, washed, left to dry with
the mustard greens, and roughly
chopped
Boiling water (enough to cover the
greens)
1 handful fresh fenugreek (methi),
washed and chopped
2 teaspoons salt (or to taste)
4 large garlic cloves, crushed
35g ginger, peeled and grated
3 green finger chillies, finely chopped
(or to taste)
100g medium cornmeal or maize flour
(be careful to read the label – this is
not the same as corn flour; you can buy
cornmeal in most good supermarkets
or Indian supermarkets)

1. Add the chopped spinach and mustard greens to a large, deep cooking pot (the greens will shrink as soon as boiling water is added so don't worry if the pot is full now).

2. Add enough boiling water to just cover the top of the vegetables. Push them down with your spoon to fully immerse them in the boiling water. Half cover and bring to the boil (this won't take long as it's already boiling water). Kamla says there should always be plenty of water in the saag to help it cook.

3. Add the fenugreek, salt, garlic, ginger and green chillies, then stir through. At this stage, it will look like a broth.

4. Half cover and simmer over a low heat for 40-45 minutes, or until the greens have softened. The pot should be really aromatic by this point.

5. Remove from the heat and use a hand-blender to blend the contents into a pulp (keep the hand-blender fully immersed so it doesn't spray out liquid).

6. Return to the hob. Stir over a high heat for 2-3 minutes, then half cover and simmer for 40-45 minutes until the liquid has reduced in the pan by about a third.

7. Mix the cornmeal with cold water in a bowl to form a medium thickness paste – this will help the saag to bind together.

8. Take the saag off the heat and carefully stir in the paste. Kamla advises to remove from the heat, because as soon as cornmeal has been added, there is an increased spitting action from the pan.

9. Still off the heat, add around 500ml of boiling water and stir well. This is needed to cook the cornmeal, so that the dish doesn't taste of raw flour.

10. Return to a low heat, half cover and simmer for 40-45 minutes until it thickens slightly. Stir occasionally during this time to check nothing is sticking (take off the heat when you stir to reduce spitting action).

11. Remove from the heat. Use a hand-blender to blend the saag again so that it becomes a smoother pulp-like consistency. Stir.

12. Simmer, uncovered, on a low heat for a further hour until a medium thickness consistency. You'll need to check on it and stir regularly to gauge how it's doing. Taste for salt during this time. The longer you can simmer it, the better. As a guide, you'll know when it's done when it comes together in one stir and has no watery bubbles around the edges of the mixture. The volume of liquid will have reduced significantly since the start of cooking. If serving saag on the day, make your tharka in a separate pan, and add as much saag as you need to the tharka.

Recipe continued overleaf.

Buying mustard greens

Saag (continued)

***To make the tharka (enough for
around 4 portions of saag):***
*1 and a half tablespoons ghee or
4 tablespoons rapeseed oil*

1 small onion, diced
2 cloves garlic, crushed
20g ginger, peeled and grated
Salt, to taste

1. Heat the ghee or oil in a saucepan. Once hot, add the onions and stir over a moderate heat.
2. Add the garlic, ginger and salt when the onions are golden brown and have softened. (If you're adding paneer or meat, add them now so that they cook through. Paneer should be uncooked and cubed when it goes in the pan, then cooked until soft.)
3. Add the saag and stir through.
4. Serve piping hot and enjoy!

Freeze note: Saag keeps well in the fridge for a few days. It also freezes well in airtight containers. For best flavour, always make a fresh tharka and re-heat in a saucepan. When defrosted, pour out excess liquid from the container. When cooking in the tharka, you will need to add a little boiling water to loosen up the saag, depending on how thick you like the consistency.

*"Traditional Punjabi saag actually
refers to a mixture of cooked leafy
green vegetables, including but not
limited to spinach. Other possible
ingredients may include mustard
greens, kale, fenugreek, broccoli,
brussels sprouts and spring greens."*

Kamla's soft fluffy rotis

Kamla has been making rotis (chapattis) with love since she was a little girl. She remembers watching the women of her village in North India using a chakki (traditional grinding stone) to grind the wholemeal wheat into flour. When her husband Jagdish was alive, he would only eat rotis which were served hot, straight off the tawa (traditional frying pan). Jagdish enjoyed his rotis just as they are traditionally eaten in India, as a staple side dish to scoop up the main dishes, or a bowl of ghiya yoghurt. Before Jagdish was married, he lived in a shared house with other men. He would resourcefully use a milk bottle to roll out his chapattis, as they didn't have a rolling pin!

In recent years, there has been a growing demand for ready-made (and frozen) chapattis, because of the technique and practice required in making them from scratch. In fact, these flatbreads, made with simple ingredients, are simple to whip up at home. Nothing beats homemade rotis with Indian food, and Kamla insists this is a skill to master.

There is a particular art to mastering soft, fluffy rotis that puff up – even though Kamla and the other dadimas in this book make it look effortless! If you've never made them before, and are hosting a dinner party, I strongly suggest that you practice them a few times beforehand. Work out a little production line so that you can have one roti at the ready whilst the other is cooking (don't stack them up – put each on a separate plate). If you're more confident, roll the next roti out whilst one is cooking. If your roti doesn't puff up, feels heavy, and is tough when torn, just keep on practicing – it's a bit like learning to ride a bike.

Chapatti flour is available in most good supermarkets. Traditionally it's made using wholemeal flour which is finely ground, but different varieties are available nowadays. Kamla always buys a medium chapatti flour (made with equal amounts of white and wholemeal flour), and as her granddaughter, I follow her lead. From speaking with the other dadimas featured in this book, I know they also prefer a medium flour for its balanced taste and texture.

If you have a dough mixer at home, it won't take long to make the atta (Punjabi for dough). If not, roll up your sleeves, grab a large mixing bowl, and knead by hand. You should prepare the dough in advance so that it has time to rest. Rotis themselves taste best served hot and freshly cooked, but not everyone is as fussy as my late grandfather.

Have fun practicing and keep going until you get your roti to 'puff up' like Kamla's!

Makes 7 rotis
300g medium chapatti flour, plus around 100g extra in a flat bowl for dusting and coating
200-210ml lukewarm water
Half teaspoon rapeseed oil, to oil the bowl in which the dough is stored
Butter, to coat the chapattis

You will need: *Small tea towel, tongs to flip the rotis, a rolling pin and a flat chapatti pan (tawa), a dough mixer if you don't want to knead by hand.*

Recipe continued overleaf.

Preparing the atta (dough):

1. If you are kneading the dough by hand, add the chapatti flour to a mixing bowl – this needs to be a large one with a wide flat base to give you room to knead (Kamla uses a stainless steel parat, a traditionally Indian wide-based shallow mixing bowl). Gradually add the water, making scooping motions around the bowl with one hand, to mix the water and flour together. You won't go wrong as long as you pour the water slowly so that you can gauge how your dough is coming together. You're looking for a texture which is firm and soft, but not sticky. If the dough is sticking to your hands too much, you'll need to add a bit more flour, but do this gradually so that you have control over the texture.

2. Time for some hardcore kneading, now that your dough is fully formed. My dadima uses a special kneading technique, taught to her by her mother, which you may want to try: make a 'thumbs-up' gesture with one hand, and clench your thumb around it with your other hand, so that your fists are locked together. Align your knuckles, and firmly rock your fists into the dough, working your way from the bottom of the dough to the top so it flattens out. It's your very own hand-rolling pin.

3. Fold the dough onto itself and repeat this rolling action 2-3 times for a soft and lump-free dough. Alternatively, use a dough mixer, observing the same principles as above.

4. Transfer your dough (atta) to a lightly oiled bowl, kneading it to fit the base of the bowl and ensuring all areas are coated in oil. This tip keeps the atta moist and easy to handle. Allow to set for a minimum of one hour in the fridge – the dough will be easier to handle and the resulting rotis will be softer.

Making the rotis:

5. Once you're ready to make your rotis, clear and prepare your workstation – a neatly laid-out space will be your safety blanket if you struggle with the roti-making technique! You need a clean, dry surface with plenty of room to roll the dough – ideally next to your cooker. Keep your flour in a wide bowl – this will make it easier when it comes to dusting. You'll also need something to put the rotis on as they come off the heat – either an insulated container, or a plate lined with kitchen roll.

6. Pre-heat your pan over a low heat whilst you roll out the rotis. If you are slower at making them, do this later. It's very important that the pan is hot before you begin.

7. Divide your dough into seven equal-sized pieces and set aside. With this quantity of dough, each piece usually weighs 70-80g. Take the first piece and roll between the palms of your hands to form a ball shape.

8. Flour coating 1: lightly coat the dough ball with flour so that it is not sticky.

9. Gently flatten the dough ball, rotating against the palm of your hands as you do so. The rotation is really important, as it helps to create an even consistency when rolling.

10. Use your rolling pin to roll the dough ball out into a small circle of about 2.5 inches diameter. Roll on one side, then flip it over and roll on the other. We can't roll it out too thinly at this stage, otherwise the dough will start sticking to the work surface and rolling pin.

11. Flour coating 2: lightly smother both sides of your roti in flour, coating all areas, ready to roll it out as thinly and evenly as possible.

Recipe continued overleaf.

Kamla's soft fluffy rotis (continued)

12. Now for rolling it out. Apply equal pressure to each rolling stroke, and use a fluid rolling motion, working from the wrists. If you apply too much pressure, the dough will stick to the surface and you'll need more flour which can create a dry, burnt effect. If the roti is uneven (i.e. too thick in places and too thin in others), it's harder to cook through and puff up. Flip using the corner of your dough and roll out again to create a large circle of around 6 inches diameter. Make sure the edges of your roti are not thick. Don't be afraid to go diagonally to make sure your dough is even. Kamla says, "as you roll, you can 'feel' if your roti is even, and this comes with practice. Thin and even rotis will puff up".

13. Place the flat roti on your hand and confidently clap it between your palms, before placing it in the centre of your hot tawa or frying pan.

14. Allow one side of the roti to heat for a few moments and then flip. Allow this other side to cook until you notice the top surface begin to show small heat bubbles and change to a light brown colour – the roti will look dry.

15. Once the browning looks evenly spread, flip the roti again using tongs (Kamla uses her hands but hers are heatproof from years of roti cooking!). If you're not sure when to flip, lift the roti up using your tongs and have a little peek at the underside – it should be light brown and may have a few brown spots.

16. When the roti starts to brown further and puff up in places, use a small tea towel to gently push the parts which have puffed up, rotating the roti around the pan as you do so. You are trying to coax the air inside all parts of the roti. Be careful – too much pressure could create a hole in the roti causing heat to escape.

17. Alternatively, at the first sign of seeing puffs of air in the roti, use tongs to place it on a naked flame – this will almost always make it puff up. Make sure air gets right into the edges of the roti so it cooks all the way through.

18. Place the roti onto a plate and smother a small knob of butter evenly over it.

19. Repeat steps 8-18 for the remaining rotis. There's no need to butter the next roti, as you're stacking it on the previously buttered roti. They only need to be buttered on one side, so butter every alternate roti if you're stacking them in this way! Serve hot with your choice of main dishes .

Prepare ahead: You can prepare the dough a few hours ahead of making rotis, or the night before for convenience. Experienced cooks like Kamla can cook rotis at speed, while the rest of the food is being heated. If you are new to making rotis, I strongly suggest that you make them ahead of your guests arriving, and keep them warm in an insulated container, or wrapped in kitchen roll and covered in foil.

"As you roll, you can 'feel' if your roti is even, and this comes with practice. Thin and even rotis will puff up."

Index

Acknowledgements

My first book fills me with appreciation for the support I have received on what was a very new and daunting journey! I believe that gratitude is one of the most rewarding feelings, and this short space cannot do justice to the thank yous I've repeated each and every day since starting dadima's.

For being my rocks throughout this journey, for encouraging me to bring the book that you hold in your hands to completion, and for supporting me when I was burning the candle at both ends, thank you to my dad, mum, and sister Tara.

For your support, positive words and listening ears, thank you to my nearest and dearest (you know who you are) for being my breath of fresh air when I was often working in isolation. I treasure every thoughtful gesture which kept me sane and pulled me away from work!

For believing in an ordinary, young girl with a big vision, thank you to those of you that have supported dadima's journey on social media. Starting small has been a lonely journey at times, and on tired evenings with my computer, a coffee and little inspiration, your comments kept my spirits high and spurred me on to complete this book.

To the talented team at RMC Media, thank you for bringing my vision to life with great dedication and care.

Thank you, Tim, for being able to capture on camera a wisdom, passion and warmth I so desperately wanted to create.

For loaning dadima's your precious space and props, thank you to the team at Elements Kitchens (Reading), Piccolino (Virginia Water), Halfords (Slough), and also to Villeroy & Boch.

Thank you, reader, for hopefully getting this book used, messy and shared with your nearest and dearest!

Thank you to the dadimas not featured in this book, who were a special part of my research, and to the wonderful cooks who advised me during this process.

Thank you to the seven beautiful dadimas in this book whose wisdom, kindness and talents will always have a special place in my heart. I enjoyed our extensive conversations over good food and lots of masala chai!

I feel truly blessed for the kindness I have received in my first publishing venture.

Enjoy cooking dadima's recipes. I hope the wisdom shared in this book inspires you to connect generations over heart-warming food and good conversation.